River Carping

River Carping

Neil Wayte

The Crowood Press

First published in 2000 by
The Crowood Press Ltd
Ramsbury, Marlborough
Wiltshire SN8 2HR

www.crowood.com

This impression 2004

© Neil Wayte 2000

British Library Cataloguing-in-Publication Data
A catalogue record for this book is available from the British Library.

ISBN 1 86126 378 3

Dedication
I would like to dedicate this book to Sharon, my wife, who has over the years of
our marriage put up with me and all the time I've spent away from home fishing.
Many wives would not have done so, let alone encouraged me.

Typeset by Naomi Lunn

Printed and bound in Great Britain by CPI Bath

Contents

Preface

Very little has been written about river carp fishing in the past, apart from odd pieces on the Thames and the Trent, but there are many more rivers in England that contain carp in such numbers that it makes fishing for them a viable proposition.

It would be very difficult to write about every river in the country that contained carp, and no angler would have enough time to fish every one and become familiar enough with each to be able to write about it. That is why I asked anglers from all over the country to write a chapter on their experiences of river carping in their area. I did not give anyone a specific brief on how to write their chapter, I just left it to them to write as they saw fit. Some describe how they approached their particular river, whilst others describe each section of the river and the size of fish you can expect to catch. Many of the authors have never written anything before and have found it difficult, but I think they have all done very well and hopefully their efforts will inspire you to look at your local running water. Many of the chapters will give you excellent starting points and tips.

A large number of modern-day carp fishing books contain pictures of huge fish that have been caught many times and have rightly or wrongly been given names. Within this book there is only one known, named fish, Dippy from the River Gipping. For myself and most of the other contributors, that is the attraction of river carping: not knowing what the next bite will bring is a tremendous thrill, along with the fact that most of the fish will never have been caught before.

River carp fishing is the last bastion of our sport in which any angler can be a pioneer, maybe not on a new river but at least on a new section of river that has never been carp fished before. Unfortunately, many of today's anglers are motivated by size and will not fish waters that do not contain thirty- or forty-pounders, or even fifty-pounders. But who is to say what size of fish a river contains if it has never been fished? To me, a mid-double is a good fish from a river, and anything above that is brilliant. What these fish lack in size they will make up for with their fighting spirit; the first river carp you hook will make you wonder what you've got on the other end, believe me.

There are a couple of chapters on drains and a chapter on canals which covers the birth of carping on this water to the present day. The dedication of the early canal carper reveals how easy we have it now. The very inclusion of drains and canals shows how widespread carp have become, meaning relatively lightly fished carp venues will not be too far away from any area of England.

Many people have helped me to compile this book, some of whom are fellow members of The British Carp Study Group, so thanks to them and to the others who encouraged me to keep on with the project when I was on the verge of giving up. Colin Davidson of *Angler's Mail* deserves a special mention for his efforts in helping me from start to finish.

Hopefully, the size of the fish in your local river will come as a surprise to you. Most of the authors have previously kept quiet about their river fishing, so all of this material is new and, I think, exciting.

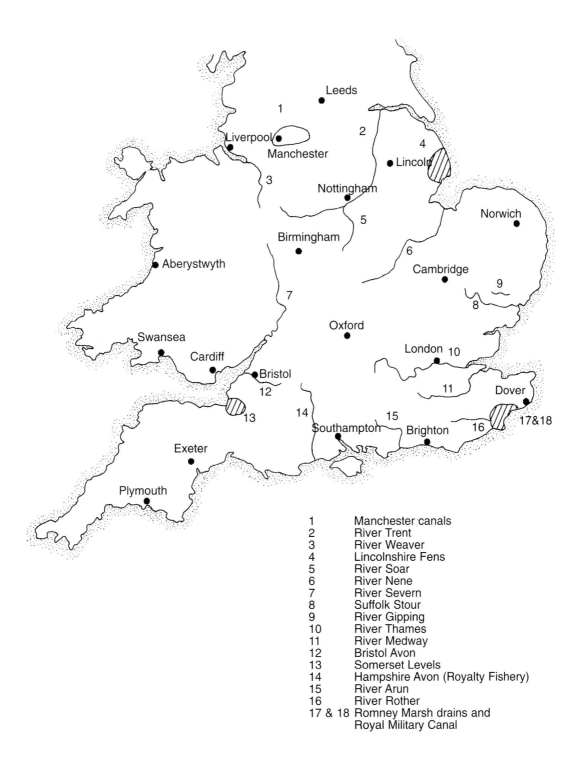

1	Manchester canals
2	River Trent
3	River Weaver
4	Lincolnshire Fens
5	River Soar
6	River Nene
7	River Severn
8	Suffolk Stour
9	River Gipping
10	River Thames
11	River Medway
12	Bristol Avon
13	Somerset Levels
14	Hampshire Avon (Royalty Fishery)
15	River Arun
16	River Rother
17 & 18	Romney Marsh drains and Royal Military Canal

1 The River Arun

Dave Eaton

Imagine you saw an advert in the angling press that read: 'Carp fishing available on an old, established, unfished water set in peaceful surroundings with carp to unknown proportions'. I would undoubtedly have to check it out, wouldn't you?

I am sure you will all agree that many waters in the south-east have become overcrowded. At weekends especially it can be very frustrating to arrive at one's chosen venue only to find the place packed with other people. You know all the decent swims will have been taken, so one has a choice: either set up and make the most of what little space there is left, or try somewhere else! I am not criticizing anglers who fish these types of waters; it seems as though the majority have come to accept the situation and are quite happy fishing in close proximity to one another. Personally, I prefer quieter waters, well away from hustle and bustle, hopefully with a touch of mystery attached – the one thing that is missing in today's carp scene. The trouble is, waters that fall into this category are becoming very hard to find.

The source of the River Arun is an amalgamation of natural springs that start deep within St Leonard's Forest to create the Hammer Ponds. The river starts its journey as a small stream, slowly increasing in size as other streams merge to create the Arun just south of Horsham. Cutting a path south through the Downs at this stage, it has grown into a powerful river, finally entering the sea at Littlehampton as one of the fastest estuaries in the country.

It was probably a natural progression for me to try to catch carp from the River Arun. Having fished it as a child I can remember spending many hours wandering about by the river. Even then I loved the excitement of casting out, not really knowing what you would catch next. The tidal Arun has always had a reputation as an inconsistent river; you could fish a particular swim in the hope of catching roach and chub and you would catch gudgeon and dace. Yet return to exactly the same spot the following day, fish with the same set-up, and catch perch, eels and even flounder on the odd occasion.

The lower stretch of the river becomes tidal and it was on this stage that I decided to concentrate my efforts. It is obvious the tide plays a major part in the movements of fish, and with a constantly changing environment they learn to adapt accordingly. Carp in particular are extremely adaptable fish as they appear to thrive in some of the most unusual places. Quite how they managed to find their way into the Arun is anyone's guess, although I know of at least one occasion when the sluice gates of one of the lakes that feed the Arun were left open overnight, only to find that by the following morning the entire contents had disappeared down the river. So where do they go? Perhaps they hole up in the deeper pools, waiting for water levels to rise, ready to move downstream hoping to find slower, more suitable conditions. The Environment Agency does stock the Arun occasionally but I doubt whether any quantities of carp have been introduced over the years.

It was by chance that I was given the opportunity to try a particular stretch that I had known about for many years but had never actually fished. I was talking to a local farmer about sea trout and how he enjoyed trying to catch them from his private stretch. Now, at that time I was into trout fishing and mentioned that I had never actually had the chance to fish for sea trout, hoping he might invite me down to have a go, which he very kindly did. What I did not realize at the time was that this generous offer would give me access to one of the most inviting-looking areas on this tidal section. In fact, it had everything you could wish for – wide sweeping bends, deep rush-lined margins, overhanging rushes and lilies – the lot. Sod the sea trout, where were the carp? The only drawback I could envisage were the young bullocks that also occupied the field, a minor problem considering the privilege.

It was not until late in the summer of 1995 that I finally had a trip down the river to have a good look around. At that time I was fishing a local lake and was struggling somewhat, as can be the case in hot weather. I am not sure what reminded me of the river but I thought then was as good a time as any to give it a try. I did not know for sure that there were any carp at all in that particular area; it just looked and felt right. I knew it would not be easy from my previous efforts at catching other species; in fact, visually locating carp of any size proved impossible. It was becoming apparent that the only way to learn their habits would be to spend some time and just fish.

You can imagine my surprise when on that first night I had a take. It took me several seconds to realize what was going on. I thought I had foul hooked a branch or weed raft by the way the rod was being wrenched round. I started to panic. There I was on my own, miles from anywhere, latched into something hell bent on putting as much distance between us as possible. Thankfully, I managed to apply enough pressure to turn the fish as it rolled about thirty yards down-

stream, just short of a large overhanging tree. Unfortunately, it was impossible to follow due to several obstacles on my own bank. So I just hung on desperately, gaining line whenever possible, and slowly but surely I managed to coax the fish up to within netting range and, with one last attempt, over she went into the net.

I could not believe my luck. I had caught a carp from the Arun at my first attempt; not a huge fish but an immaculate common weighing just over 14lb. The power and determination were quite remarkable; in fact, I was concerned as to how I would manage to control anything larger should I be lucky enough to hook one.

This first capture made me wonder how many carp might be present. There could be a lot more fish than I had hoped for – or was it just a fluke? With all these questions and more to answer I couldn't wait to get back down and have another session.

The following day I was telling my friend, Andy, about the weekend's events and suggested he might like to join me. I knew he would like the peace and quiet if nothing else. Like myself, Andy had fished some pretty obscure places over the years and enjoyed a good challenge. At the time he was fishing a large pit down on the south coast and doing very well catching several big fish by stalking, but decided to pull off due to holidaymakers making a nuisance of themselves. So the weekend could not come quick enough.

We decided to fish the same area from Saturday evening through until Sunday lunchtime. I can remember the look on Andy's face as we approached the swims. The river was carrying about three feet of extra water and was hacking through at an incredible pace.

'Are you sure about this, Dave?' he asked.

All I could say was, 'Sorry but it wasn't like this last week!'

The flow wasn't the problem, it was the amount of debris being washed down. It

Andy Skinner with a typical River Arun common.

must have looked comical, the pair of us constantly recasting every few minutes, pulling weed from the lines. Even if there had been carp present I am sure after we had finished they would have well and truly disappeared.

It was not surprising we blanked but we learnt some very important lessons that weekend. On our next trip we resolved some of the problems of presentation. The tide was nowhere near as strong as the previous week which made things a lot easier. Andy continued fishing with a tight line direct to the lead, keeping as much line as possible out of the water, whereas I tried clipping on a small backlead to change the angle of line from rod top to bait. Andy's method appeared to be ideal when fishing across to the far margin, and the backlead proved excellent from the centre into our own margin. We both felt a lot more confi-

dent being able to position baits and leave them undisturbed for much longer periods. We could now concentrate on solving some of the other problems associated with not only moving water but continuously changing depths. Depending at what level the tide was and how much rainwater had entered the system, the difference could be as much as six or seven feet over the tide change, even in summer!

Our persistence and hard work were rewarded. Andy caught a beautiful fish on what was our third session: a mirror at 14lb and without doubt never having seen a hook before. We did not experiment with terminal rigs, varying only hook link lengths and the amount of lead needed to hold bottom. We used very simple set-ups; there seemed no point in overcomplicating things unnecessarily – the more we fished the more our confidence grew. We hoped a pattern would emerge regarding feeding spells. It was obvious that at high tide species like roach and dace became more active; they would start topping, which in turn would encourage the pike to feed.

We hoped the carp's feeding habits might be influenced in the same way. Making sure everything was in position just prior to the slack period, even in the hours of darkness if we were awake, we both felt our chances increased within this turning point so we tried to calculate the tide patterns using time charts, bearing in mind the area we fished was about ten miles from the estuary. We clearly needed to spend as much time as possible actually fishing if we were to stand any chance of catching one of the bigger fish we felt it could produce.

So the following weekend we set up on our usual stretch. Andy was on the bend fishing across to the rushes, whilst I had chosen to fish downstream. I felt confident in this area having caught there before. Directly across the river an inlet was pushing through, creating a large back eddy as it entered the main flow. So my first bait was flicked out to this spot where the currents met. The trouble was, where to put the second bait? I finally decided to fish just in front of a large overhanging bush, an area that looked more likely to hold chub than carp. I had just finished putting some free baits out when I heard a strange clicking noise. As I looked up, the right-hand rod was arched over. I had forgotten to turn the alarm on. As I picked up the rod Andy appeared.

'What's up mate, are you in that snag again?'

'No, I have got one on and it feels like a good fish,' was my response.

This fish did not run in the same way as previous fish, it just hugged the bottom and swam around in a large circle shaking its head. Gradually I managed to pump the fish up to the surface and Andy did the honours with the net. I could tell it was a good fish as he struggled to lift it clear. As we unfolded the net we were amazed by the size of the tail. After the usual weighing and photographing we returned a beautiful mirror of 19lb.

I was understandably delighted. The problem was, it blew our high-tide theory out of the water. Not only was it hooked within two minutes of casting out in daylight, but the tide had turned and had been pushing in rapidly. For the rest of the afternoon we sat up on the flood bank in between our swims, overlooking the whole river and checking for any signs of carp feeding on our baits.

Suddenly Andy whispered, 'Look, straight out in front, just below the surface.'

I scanned the area but could not see anything. He threw over his Polaroids to eliminate the surface glare. Just as I stood up it came into view and very gently this huge pair of white lips broke the surface and sucked down a floating leaf. We both stood there silent with big grins on our faces. It is always difficult to judge the weight of any carp in the water, especially when it is murky, but this fish looked considerably bigger than the nineteen-pounder I had caught earlier in the day. We did fire out a few floaters in the hope of enticing it back up to the surface, but only succeeded in attracting the attentions of our feathered friends. This was the first positive sighting we had witnessed apart from captures since we had started, and it really fired our imaginations regarding the size of the fish that might be present in the river.

Winter was fast approaching and the tidal Arun floods without warning at this time of year, so we felt we had to make the most of what little time we had left. I had decided on a mid-week session, arriving just before daybreak. The river was high and really pushing through due to the recent rain, and after several casts it became apparent that I would need to increase the lead size from 1oz to 2oz to hold bottom. So I positioned

Another run on the Arun; Dave Eaton with a 19lb 8oz mirror.

the baits out and sat back to enjoy the scenery. I must have nodded off because I was abruptly awoken by four bullocks that had chosen my swim for a drink, although I doubt whether this disturbance affected the fishing in any way.

After some gentle persuasion with a big stick I finally managed to get rid of them and get back into my angling. Time for a recast, so out went two baits in similar positions to before and the third rod was baited with an old bait I had found lurking at the bottom of my rucksack. Why I proceeded to use one of these rock hard baits from the previous winter I am not sure. I chucked this bait down the edge, close to a large weedbed. The rest of the afternoon passed without any action, plus the tide had bottomed out, and I was just considering packing up when one of the rod tips pulled round and stopped. Without hesita-

tion I picked up the rod and struck into something that turned in the current and very slowly headed upstream. I had no choice but to follow it and hang on. I gave that fish as much pressure as the gear would allow but still I could not make an impression on it. It stopped in the main flow as if thinking what to do next, and bolted straight into a snag with incredible power.

I was gutted. I knew I had hooked something special that had beaten me. I will never forget that evening and the circumstances in which I hooked that fish. I have never before felt such power from a carp – if indeed it was a carp. That was to be the last action on the river that season. Andy caught another small common the following weekend but the river burst its banks shortly afterwards and put an end to a most enjoyable season.

I personally think that the abolition of the

close season was a mistake. Most sports seem to benefit from a break of some kind, especially angling, where we have to take into account the impact on our environment. The old system gave wildlife a brief period of recovery. So I am more than happy to keep the close season on our river systems.

It was still the close season when we started a prebaiting campaign on the river with roughly two kilos of bait per week, half of which was introduced mid-week and the remainder when we fished. We both felt that the previous autumn's results could be improved with time and regular baiting. Finally, 16 June arrived. I could not take the day off as it was one of the busiest times in the shop where I was working, so we set off after I had closed up, not minding too much and knowing we would have virtually the whole river to ourselves. In fact, we felt sorry for other anglers that weekend, cramming themselves in wherever possible.

The anticipation and excitement as we tackled up that evening was fantastic. We had just finished getting everything in position and were enjoying a much needed drink when a large carp turned over right in front of us. We sat there, our eyes glued to the indicators, willing one of them to jump into life.

Suddenly my middle indicator rose steadily. I picked up the rod and felt the satisfying thump of a good fish after a dogged and powerful scrap. Andy slipped the net under what proved to be a very good fish. What a start! First cast on the first day of a new season and a gorgeous 25lb 2oz mirror. Our theory had been confirmed: the Arun was capable of producing large carp.

It's difficult to describe the pleasure derived from catching a carp from the river. All the planning, prebaiting and countless hours spent sitting behind motionless rods pays off when you do finally land one. Our river systems have a great deal to offer the carp angler who is prepared to make the effort and try something different.

Finally, don't forget: 'Of man's allotted span, time spent fishing is not deducted...'

2 The Hampshire Avon Royalty Fishery

Andy Sloane

The Royalty Fishery on the Hampshire Avon at Christchurch in Dorset was acquired by the West Hampshire Water Company in 1929. Prior to this it had passed into private ownership through a direct grant from the English Crown before the Magna Carta in around AD1215. References to a Royal Fishery at Christchurch date back to AD939.

It appears that the title 'Royalty Fishery' was conferred by royal grant in the reign of Queen Mary and renewed by Elizabeth I in the sixteenth century, the Fishery having devolved to the Crown by forfeiture for treason. It lies within the Avon Valley Site of Special Scientific Interest and is an integral part of the designation.

The Royalty is based at the lower end of one of southern England's best chalk streams, the Hampshire Avon, and provides over a mile of double-bank fishing. The fishery holds a wide variety of species, including barbel, chub, dace, roach, pike, perch, bream, salmon, sea trout, tench and, of course, carp.

I went to the Royalty for the first time with a school friend at the age of eleven and was completely captivated by the whole aura of the place. I knew from that day that it was where I'd learn the art of fishing, amongst some of the best anglers in the business. I would keep my mouth shut and my eyes open, watching various anglers and their different methods, but the only downside was that I couldn't afford the tackle that most of them used. I envied people with their split-cane rods, such as the Richard Walker MkIV Avon and Aerial centrepins, and put up with the cheap and cheerful tackle bought by my parents. Since that year I have never missed 16 June, right up to the present day. Even at school, because of my obsession with the river my mum would let me be 'sick' for the day and I would sneak off down to the Royalty for another session trying to catch barbel and chub.

I started to become more successful around the age of fifteen, capable of catching most river species, and although there were no big fish I was fairly consistent. On the first day of the 1986 season I caught a 9lb 3oz mirror, my first ever carp, while tench fishing in The Backwater. I was absolutely amazed; the notion of carp in the Avon seemed crazy at the time. I thought I'd caught the only carp in the river, but the following month I was fortunate enough to land another two fish, one to sweetcorn and the other to slow-sinking bread bait. Both fish were beautiful commons of 8lb 8oz and 7lb 10oz respectively. The captures were largely thanks to Dick Dakin, a good friend and long-time honorary bailiff at the Royalty. He had a vast knowledge of the river and taught me a lot about laying on techniques. With such good presentation I could suddenly catch the elusive carp.

To be perfectly honest, I didn't really see much more in the way of carp on The Backwater for a number of years, and I suppose I was drawn back to the barbel in the main river, fishing amongst the likes of Ray Walton and Chris Holley. I used to watch them roll meat, making it look quite easy when others like myself would struggle to bend the rod.

Because I was on the river probably more than I was at home, Head Bailiff Alan Godfrey asked me if I would be interested in working as a bailiff on the fishery full time. It was an absolute dream come true, and of course he didn't have to twist my arm too much for me to say yes! So on 6 March 1989, at nineteen years old, I started my first day's work on the Royalty as assistant bailiff. Alan showed me the ropes, and how to maintain the high standards expected of one of the most prestigious fisheries in the country. He had vast knowledge, passed down from other bailiffs over the years, and used to tell me stories about the old times and pass on tips on certain swims and techniques. One of his famous sayings was: 'No matter how many years you're here, you never know it all.' Never a truer word was spoken, because every season, whether high water or low water, features change and swims alter for better or worse.

After 1990, a lot of rivers throughout the country were desperate for water due to low levels of rainfall in the spring, and the winters becoming increasingly mild. When the summer came it was very hot and rivers were choked with weed. The low levels were having quite an effect on flow rates, and areas of golden gravel were becoming quite heavily silted. I can even recall taking the water temperature at an amazing 76° Fahrenheit one particular day. As you can imagine, to most freshwater fish this would be like swimming in a hot bath. However, there was one fish that didn't seem to mind these extreme conditions, and that, of course, was the carp. As I carried out my work duties they could be seen throughout the whole river. They appeared to thrive in any swim, even in the fastest-flowing reaches of the water and in amongst barbel shoals as though they had been used to it for years, not batting an eyelid about competing for food on the gravel glides.

So where did the Royalty carp come from? Speaking to one or two anglers, they recalled catching a few carp in the late 1970s, up to around 3lb. I have also heard of pike anglers using them as livebait and at the end of the day tipping the remaining fish into the river, maybe not realizing that the little beauties would grow and grow.

Another story was that once, when the Avon was in flood, some carp escaped from a pond further upstream and came down south to the lower reaches, stopping in the Royalty waters because the next stage is the sea. It is quite possible that most of the carp came from the New Forest ponds, which have a good head of carp and also tench. The Backwater, which is like a pond, is part of the river, full of lily pads and fed by a stream which comes from the Forest. Again, when in flood, small carp and also tench could have been washed down to the Avon. I have caught plenty of tench over the years and no one has ever explained how they got there in the first place.

Some anglers have even confessed to parking on the road bridge, purposely putting small carp into The Backwater. The pool always looked very carpy and, like myself, maybe other anglers just loved the species and hoped that one day in the future they might be a nice size to fish for.

SWEET 16 JUNE

Whilst walking down The Backwater on a warm sunny day during the close season in May 1993, I was astounded at the number of carp swimming frantically all over the pool, chasing each other in a frenzy. Putting two and two together, I realized that spawning wasn't far away. I just sat mesmerized because the pool was full of fish of all sizes, from, I would guess, 6lb to over 20lb. That afternoon I came back with a loaf of bread and threw in a few slices. The fish went ballistic, eating it as if it was Christmas. They looked absolutely beautiful, feeding like koi, totally oblivious to me and swimming

Andy Sloane with a River Avon 30lb mirror.

so gracefully right under the bank by my feet. I think it was at that moment that I decided river carp were for me, and that it would be nice to go for a species that not too many people had pursued, and catch fish of a quality that had never been on the bank before.

A couple of days went by and it was still very warm. Spawning started, and they completely trashed the lilies, males chasing females on the surface, mirrors, commons and what looked like a number of near leathers all involved in a mass orgy. This frenzied activity continued into June, mainly in the afternoons. I was beginning to feel my adrenalin start to rise as the magical 16th grew nearer; for the first time ever the start would see me fishing for carp instead of barbel.

A week before the season I purchased a new rod, a Bruce & Walker Ray Walton Specialist 1lb test curve, a fantastic rod designed to perfection for the Royalty. Designed for rolling meat it has similar characteristics to split cane in many ways, despite being made from carbon and filled with foam. I intended to break the rules slightly and use it for those carp on opening day because I had faith in its supreme power and I loved its through action.

Well, the kick-off to the 1993 season arrived and everybody stayed on the main river, leaving the Backwater empty. At four in the afternoon, I started to make my way to the intended swim, travelling light and sticking with a roving approach, just as if I was barbel fishing the main river. The tackle was simple – rod, reel, 10lb line and a size four hook, a small bag carrying a few odds and ends like forceps, scales, weigh sling and a loaf of bread, not forgetting the Polaroids and a net – two vital pieces of kit, especially when fishing for the big boys.

It did seem a lot quieter when I got there, as if they all knew it was 16 June, but I noticed some pads move on the far side so I headed in that direction, treading very quietly and slowly crouching in the bankside cover. As I put on a piece of uncut loaf it reminded me of catching my first three Avon carp, which seemed like many years ago. This time there were a lot more – and a lot bigger – fish. The pads shimmered and the excitement started to flow as I lowered the bread on to the surface, trying not to spook the fish below the rod tip.

Near on instantly a pair of big rubber lips sucked in the bread, and before I knew it there was an explosion on the surface and my reel was screaming. After the first run I worked the fish to the net, and after a minute or so landed a mint condition common that weighed 9lb 7oz. Still not a double, but I was pleased with a perfect specimen that had probably never seen a hook in its entire life. After a four-hour session I ended up with two fish, the other a mirror at 6lb 8oz. I felt quite pleased, the common having set a new personal best. A few days later I took another mirror on float-fished corn at 7lb 1oz, and then The Backwater went very quiet as if all the carp had disappeared into the main river.

On 29 June I was doing my rounds checking tickets, heading towards the famous

21lb mirror carp.

Railway Swim. Peering into the slack water I noticed more carp and decided to give them a go after work. I could hear distinct slurping noises coming from the weedbed and then I noticed what I call humping. The weed was extremely thick but I thought I'd go for it. The humping was due to the carp sieving through the surface for food, or sunbathing, causing the weedbed to rise on its back; if you knew where to look, sometimes it was a complete giveaway. Once again I lowered the floating crust into unknown territory, this time on the river itself, not really knowing what reaction I would get in what some people would think an unnatural environment for carp. Sure enough, the take was almost instant, but I got smashed up almost immediately. I was completely gutted, to say the least. I knew that fish was bigger than anything I had ever caught.

Annoyed with myself for losing it and thinking I had spooked the whole area, I set up a rolling meat rig and tried for barbel. I moved around the pool just a few feet to cast, and then saw three large shapes swimming upstream. With the Polaroids I could see they were about twenty feet from this huge weedbed, so I cast in front of them. The meat started sinking and the smallest shape moved towards it. The take was similar to a bream, but when I struck all hell let loose, the fish tearing up into Greenbanks. I just leant into it and after about five minutes it started to weaken. I could sense this was no nine-pounder and felt myself starting to shake with anticipation. A thick raft of weed floating downstream covered the fish, and seemed to have a calming effect on it as it stopped thrashing around. I remember being told that it was like an old trick used on big spring salmon.

Just a yard from the net it wallowed one last time and I lowered it straight into the net, more or less lifting it out all in one motion. This felt better than anything I had ever landed before, and as I pulled back the weed there it was, a superb 22lb 8oz mirror

caught on 10lb line with a four hook using meat. My personal best was shattered and, funnily enough, my first double-figure carp was taken on probably one of the last baits I personally would use for carp on the Royalty. At the time I would never have imagined I could beat this fish again, but nevertheless my determination to catch more of the leviathans from the deep grew.

Now the more serious approach was under way and my success rate was improving season to season between June and November. I preferred to stalk my quarry and then fish because I found it far more rewarding than fishing blind. It was exciting to see a shoal of carp intercept your bait, and seeing the take was second to none. The doubles started flowing, with fish taking bread on the surface and on the bottom, right under the bank or even in the centre of the river on a clear day. I started working out feeding times and could more or less catch to order on the right week. Five o'clock seemed to ring the dinner bell in the Railway Slack. The Railway Pool was my favourite swim, although one day in the Parlour Pool produced four doubles, all taken on crust off the surface.

My carping on the Royalty consisted of short sessions of between one to three hours because of work or home commitments. But I could see how some carp fishermen ended up divorced because of their obsession with the species, as I have never known any other fish to have the same effect on people. As I am writing this chapter I am tempted to give it another go tonight!

On 13 October 1994 I decided to fish the Top Piles, a swim on which I had spotted carp close to the bank. I was fishing with Dick Dakin and hadn't had a sniff all evening as I was using corn rather than the usual Mother's Pride. As the season progressed I found that bread became useless and I thought I'd give corn a go for old times' sake. Still nothing. Dick said to try a lobworm, this being his favourite for many

22lb 4oz common carp.

years, so I did just that. Growing out of a hole in the Piles was a small alder tree, so fishing over depth with a float and a huge lobworm and sweetcorn cocktail I cast under the tree. After about twenty minutes the float slid away into the deepest part of the fishery and I struck hard. After a superb scrap I landed a common of 20lb on the nose, and in absolutely pristine condition – the best common up to that point and the most treasured fish of my life. Some of these carp fight like Trojans and the first run is awesome as they tear off like a bull in a china shop.

A definite pattern was starting to appear: fishing The Backwater early season until the end of the first week in July was about right. After that, the carp would make their way on their migratory paths up the main river. The Backwater seemed to be the main spawning ground, but although fish could be found there all year round, the fish that remained were usually small. By late July The Backwater was normally choked with weed and pads due to the strong sunlight.

The best two carp I landed on The Backwater were an 18lb 8oz mirror in 1995 on floating crust, and a 17lb common in 1996 on slow-sinking bread. On my most successful day I took six carp, totalling just over 81lb, all on bread, which was a great feat when fishing amongst carp still spawning. In fact, whilst I was landing some of them, spawning fish were following the hooked fish into the landing net. I had never seen anything like it in my life; I wish I had it all on film.

THE BAIT I LOVED TO HATE

In October 1995 I was making it clear to all my friends that there was one bait I could not stand: the boilie. I'd never even used one, let alone bought a packet, but I knew their reputation and how deadly they could be from reading the angling press. Somehow I always thought they were nothing but bad news for the health of the carp, but after looking into it there did not seem to be a problem. A carp angler visiting the Royalty that year was using boilies and had some fabulous carp, some around the 25lb mark. He became a good friend and showed me how to fish the boilie his way. The river had coloured up due to heavy rain, and visibility was not good, so on 9 November I used my first boilie and caught an 11lb common from the swim called The Trammels.

There was no doubt about it, the boilies were fetching a better class of fish, and the strawberry flavour, which were red in colour, became a sort of sweet; it was like feeding candy to a baby. By the end of July I had caught thirty-four carp, including twenty-six doubles, since the day I got the Hexagraph rod back in 1993. On a few occasions I was smashed by the odd fish and decided to step up to 12lb line. The river weed could be so tough sometimes, and I found that 10lb was man enough on a good day, but 12lb very rarely let me down. Different flavoured boilies were successful too, taking fish from all over the river.

17lb common.

A RIVER THIRTY

One afternoon in late September I was doing my normal duty, checking permits, and walked upstream, scanning the usual haunts for carp in the Rannunculus weedbeds. At that time of year it is not unusual to see carp right under the water's edge, either sunbathing or looking for some loose offerings of food. I am always amazed at the number of anglers who walk the bank looking in the middle of the river, but never actually look under the bank. Another tip when the river is gin clear is to look for cloudy or very dirty water. Walk upriver and more often than not you will see a carp feeding away, totally oblivious to everything around it.

The day was very mild and the carp active throughout the upper reaches of The Trammels, clouding the bottom in between large bream shoals. Continuing around the Top Weir, now going down the West Bank alongside the Parlour Pool, I approached some anglers at the popular swim called Watersmeet. After checking their permits I started to pick up some litter left by careless people who were at the swim earlier that morning. Several yards below Watersmeet there is a group of crack willows and alders. Between the trees the bankside growth is quite dense with willow herb sedges and reeds. I could see more litter that had become clogged in the bottom of the vegetation, so I crouched down to pick it up. It wasn't a swim I really took much notice of, but on this day, for some unknown reason, I stood on a tree stump and looked over the reeds. The swim was untouched, although not surprisingly as it was choked with weed and not really the ideal swim for barbel fishing. Because I always wear Polaroids not much escapes my attention, and under the weed I could see dark shadows moving slowly away about two yards from the bank.

Standing motionless for about ten minutes, it all became quite clear. They were commons, but not of average size. They were all monsters. Some people who recognized me started to walk over so I distracted them away from the swim as if nothing was there at all. With hindsight this would seem a little selfish; however, I badly wanted to give these fish a crack, knowing that maybe something a bit special was down there.

I carried on checking permits and ended up back at the office for a cup of tea, pondering an approach to outwit them. I remembered a small patch of exposed gravel, totally clean of debris, with a gentle flow of water coming from the Parlour about eighteen inches from the bank. Boilies were on the menu because they could create a good scent trail and draw fish from the Pipe swim, especially if any were lurking down there. Carp were often spotted around the Pipes and my guess was that these fish were probably the very same.

Now and then fishermen would hook a fish and get smashed in the Pipes, claiming it was the biggest barbel known to man. I would laugh to myself, knowing that he had obviously hooked a carp on 6lb line and tried to put the brakes on, failing miserably. The line I was planning to use was 12lb, with the usual size four Drennan Boilie Hook with a hair of three-round monofilament just tied in at the eye of the hook.

All set and ready to go, I walked to the swim and crouched down behind the reeds to stop the sun casting my shadow across the river. Trying not to spook anything that was there I gently threw some scopex boilies on to the gravel bed, convincing myself this had to be the taking spot, or the plate as some people call it. Putting a 20mm bait on, I lowered it between the free offerings and sat patiently for about an hour with no sign of activity. The sun continued to move around, now leaving very little of my shadow over the pool. Looking through the reeds, carp appeared from nowhere, and before I could blink the reel was screaming from the ratchet. After a superb fight I banked a glorious 21lb 8oz common, an absolutely mint condition specimen. I quickly returned it to the water downstream. Recovering instantly, it swam towards the Pipes. Absolutely ecstatic I cast back in straight away, quite content with that fish even if it was the only one for the week.

Sitting down to relax, the rod butt sprang into the air with another fish on it. Leaping to my feet with a firm grip on the rod I netted it instantly. Not only did I surprise myself, but the carp must have been amazed how quickly it was landed. I couldn't believe it – another beauty at 20lb 8oz, again in fabulous condition. Two twenty-pounders in ten minutes, what more could I ask for?

A friend of mine was as stunned as I was, especially given the disturbance from the first fish, but nevertheless it just showed the potential of the carping on the Royalty. No more action followed, and as sunset came I prebaited with more boilies to keep the others interested. Just before leaving I looked out across the river and saw a huge shape heading upstream at the tail end of five or six commons. The light was poor and I could not quite make out the size of this fish. A gut feeling told me this was what I'd been looking for and I was eager to return the following day. When the next day came, however, I had other commitments, and I felt sick as a parrot, knowing that this elusive specimen was out there.

JUDGEMENT DAY

The following evening my pulse was racing with excitement as I made my way to the swim that had given me such a fantastic evening's sport two days earlier. Slowly approaching the hotspot, I once again looked over the reeds; the gravel bar was free of loose offerings prebaited the day before. I did notice some resident coots take quite a liking to boilies, no matter what flavour they were, but in the back of my mind I knew of only one reason for the lack of boilies – the carp.

Looking in my bag I noticed all the scopex boilies were gone, but I had a packet of the old faithful 20mm strawberry baits. Throwing a few loose baits in, I proceeded to check every knot and make sure the hook was razor sharp, a very important procedure when fishing heavily weeded swims in the fast-flowing water. It was about 6pm when once again the bait was lowered in, ready to ambush the quarry.

Leaning against a tree which gave me a clear view of the swim and also great cover, I saw no sign of fish and started to get a bit despondent, thinking there were no carp there at all. After forty minutes, still scanning the area, I caught sight of the first carp in the middle of the river. Knowing that they don't patrol alone, I had the feeling that more would show very soon. I crouched down and fixed my eyes on the bait below. The thick weedbed at the tail end of the baited area shimmered, an effect I call 'nervous water'. To me it could only spell one thing: carp.

Eagerly waiting, I watched a bow wave pushing its way upstream and the tension was unbelievable. Suddenly two commons appeared, jostling for the red strawberry boilies. There was a huge commotion and the commons parted, making way for a massive mirror which filled the entire gravel patch. My hands were shaking and I ducked down, looking through the reeds, when a tail like a builder's shovel came to the surface. Within the blink of an eye the rod catapulted into the air, ripping its way through the reeds. In full flight I dived and caught the last inch of the butt and the ratchet screamed as the fish went downstream like a scalded cat.

An 18½lb mirror caught with a floating crust.

The run was at least forty yards and my index finger was in pain because of the sheer power of the fish; the friction from the spool was burning my finger. From where I was standing there was no way I could get the fish back, so I climbed around the trees. By this time it was near the Pipes swim. Running down the bank, trying to get as much line back on the reel as possible, I bent the rod into this awesome fish. The rod was tip to butt and the line started singing under the immense pressure, but I was making no progress. Several anglers were running down the bank because they recognized the ratchet on my reel making the noise everyone loves to hear. At that point the pressure was definitely on, as not only did I have this monster attached, I also had several spectators. Still making no progress, and with unbelievable strain on the rod, the fish surfaced in the middle of the river creating a huge vortex of water. It was the closest thing to a spring salmon, and I knew this was the largest fish of my life. This was the time

when testing the knots, hooks and line, combined with a decent rod and reel, would prove so vital.

The carp started to wallow in the middle of the river and suddenly a fisherman jumped in wearing chest waders. Another angler passed him the net and I remember saying, 'Don't stab at it, let me lower it in,' feeling so nervous I could hardly contain myself. The 12lb line I was using was at the limit and I was praying it would not give way. With the fish in the centre of the river and the fast-flowing water it felt as though I had hooked the QE2 cruise liner.

The angler with the net had the best view of the carp as he waded towards it pushing the net into the water. I started to walk the fish upstream and she didn't resist at all. He then yelled, 'It's massive!' Having seen so many fish lost at the net over the years I was praying he would not ruin this dream I had so long awaited.

The next moment the carp was netted perfectly and I cannot explain the relief I felt as he started wading towards me. I don't know who was more excited, him or me. He looked to be in deep shock, gazing into the net as he passed it to me. I grabbed the rim and pulled it up the bank, realizing it felt like a ton weight. There was not only the fish in there, but half the river's weed. I brushed it aside, and there lay a whopping great mirror. Weighing the fish on two sets of scales it was an amazing 30lb 1oz, and I can tell you I was the happiest person in England that evening. The fish was returned to the water and after about a minute it was out of sight, on its way to join the rest of its posse and live for another day. It had shoulders like Arnold Schwarzenegger and you could see the power it had from the size of the wrist of the tail. It was truly a magnificent specimen and could easily earn the right to be called The King of the River.

Since my carp quest began in 1993, to August 1998, I banked eighty carp, including one thirty-pounder and fourteen twenties. The average weight is about 16lb and on warm summer evenings I have tempted fish to 22lb on floating crust.

A FEW POINTERS

I would advise the use of a minimum of 10lb line to combat the thick weedbeds and the hard-fighting carp in the fast-flowing water of the Hampshire Avon. Bolt rigs are not necessary in rivers so the rig is a running ledger, a very successful method, tried and tested on all swims. Hook size is a personal choice, but I prefer to use a size four no matter which method I use for fishing carp.

Watercraft and experience are essential to achieve good results. Probably 80 per cent of my fish have been caught through observation. If more time is spent looking rather than fishing, a distinct pattern of feeding times and patrol routes will become apparent on each visit to the venue.

Carp on the Royalty are very nomadic and will go to the River Stour or even Christchurch Harbour. So when the going gets tough it might be worth looking a mile downstream.

Polaroids are vital for stalking. They also reduce the strain on your eyes when scanning the water for several hours, especially on a bright summer day.

Travel as light as possible. On the Royalty, the use of bivvies and bite alarms is not necessary. Even when carrying a rod rest, I slide it into the butt of my landing net handle to make life a little easier.

I firmly believe that a carp will take any bait, if presented properly. Put in small amounts of loose offerings regularly on several swims and rotate them through the day and sooner or later one will be occupied. It has worked on countless occasions in the past, and travelling light will definitely help avoid blank days.

On some swims the unhooking mat is needed to avoid any harm coming to the fish. If carp are captured and damaged in any way, the use of antiseptic such as Kryston Klinik is ideal for sores and abrasions to give them a helping hand towards a full recovery.

And finally... if a monster river carp is one of your goals, the Royalty Fishery has to be amongst the top venues for the future. It really does have so much to offer, with fine specimens that are in the best of health and fight like Trojans.

3 The Hampshire Avon in Winter

Neil Wayte

This small piece is a follow-on from Andy Sloane's chapter on 'The Hampshire Avon Royalty Fishery' and covers my own experiences there during the winter of 1998.

Most of Andy's fishing is done up to October, when the river colours up, stopping him from spotting fish before he targets them. I had been intending to go down and fish with Andy all summer but hadn't got round to it, so when I phoned and said that I would be coming down in November

he was a little sceptical, saying that I had left it a bit late in the year to start on the Royalty. Having only spoken to Andy on the phone I wanted to meet him anyway, so I made the long trip along the south coast one wet Saturday morning.

I had fished the Royalty many years before but I could not visualize the river at all, and I was surprised when, on arriving, myself and Dave Eaton were the only ones waiting for the gates to be opened at

Neil Wayte with a 23lb 8oz common caught on the River Avon in winter.

7.30am. Andy had promised to meet us there and point us in the right direction, but anyone who knows Andy will know that getting up in the morning is not his strong point, so after waiting for a few minutes I made my way along the river looking for a bit of slack water to fish. The river was high and belting through, so anywhere out of the main flow had to be a good bet. The swim I finally decided on was known as the Railway Slack, situated just above the railway line that crosses the river.

Both rods were cast along the edge of the weedbed in the near margin and I hedged my bets with bait and fished one on luncheon meat and the other on Richworth Esterberry boilies. If the carp didn't want to feed, at least I had the chance of a barbel, a fish I have never caught. Nothing happened for a couple of hours and then on the far bank somebody waved at me. I guessed it was Andy. He made his way round to me and said that I was fishing the second best spot for carp but that I should really be up at Watersmeet, a swim below the famous Parlour Pool.

As we stood talking, a gust of wind turned my umbrella inside out, which Andy said was a sign that we should retire to his rod room for a cup of tea. We must have spent an hour talking and eventually the rain died off and the sun came out. This was my cue to move up to Watersmeet.

By the time I got fishing again it must have been around midday. The baits remained the same and were fished across the river to the slack water at the end of the Parlour Pool where the two parts of the river join up again. I sat watching the tips of the rods as they moved with the current; every now and then they would bounce as a piece of weed hit the line.

Around one o'clock the left-hand rod tip slammed down and the Baitrunner was spinning. I struck immediately and had to give line straight away as the fish headed off up the Parlour. Its next trick was to turn round and try to get into the fast water of the main river. My Armalite was bent into a horrifying curve as I tried to stop this downstream rush. My luck held and as the fish came back upstream I could see a golden flank deep down in the water. I thought I had hooked a big barbel, and when it quickly rolled on the surface I was still convinced it was a barbel on the end. Eventually the fish tired and surfaced on the edge of the weeds in front of me. Barbel my foot – it was a great big common. Luckily I had invested in an extending landing net handle so I could reach it without bringing it through the weeds.

What a start to my winter's fishing on the Royalty – a common of 23lb 8oz. A new personal best and the biggest carp I had caught from a river. The fish had its revenge, however, because as I went to put it back I stepped in a hole and fell in, much to the amusement of the small group of onlookers.

I rebaited and recast, replacing the luncheon meat on one rod with an Esterberry boilie, and around each hook-bait I threw in another ten boilies. Every time the rod top knocked I nearly jumped off my chair, but nothing else happened until packing up time, which in the winter is around 4.15pm. I picked up the right-hand rod to wind in, only to feel a bump on the tip. I struck. The rod was nearly pulled out of my hand, and out in the swim a big common rolled on the surface at exactly the same time as the hook pulled. Normally I would have sworn, but I'd had all the luck I deserved with the twenty-three-pounder.

My initial thoughts were that I had been extremely lucky catching first time down, but that did not stop me from planning my next trip. Due to family commitments and the fact that it cost around £35 a trip, I did not return until the middle of December. I had been on the phone to Andy constantly in the meantime, asking all sorts of questions and enquiring as to whether anybody else had been carp fishing. Nobody else had and nothing much was being caught, but my enthusiasm was such that I was having trouble sleeping. Most people wouldn't understand, but I'm sure that anglers will.

On arrival I bought my day ticket from Davis Angling and headed up the river to Watersmeet like a man possessed. There were two other anglers in front of me and I was worried they would go to the swim I wanted. Luckily they set up in the Pipes swims.

Putting my gear down at the top of the bank I set up both rods and baited both with Esterberries, set up the landing net and put the bank sticks in. The first rod was cast towards the big willow on the end of the island and after I had tightened the line I switched the buzzer on. I had twenty or so baits in my pocket so I threw these out and turned round to pick up the second rod, but before I could do so the buzzer bleeped a couple of times and as I turned to look the Baitrunner started clicking. It took a little while for me to realize what was going on, but when I struck there was no doubt what was attached to the other end.

Another mighty battle took place before I was able to net another cracking common. This one was not as big as the November fish, but at 19lb 12oz and immaculate who worries about a couple of ounces?

The two anglers setting up in the Pipes could not believe I'd caught so quickly, and in truth neither could I, but in the middle of winter any chance is most welcome. I sat glued to the rods for the rest of the day but without any more action. After the early success I was convinced I was going to bag up, but that was just being greedy.

By now I couldn't get enough of the Avon; it was just a shame that it was 130 miles from home. I decided that it would be a good idea to invite some of the other British Carp Study Group members down for a day's fishing so we pencilled it in for the middle of January. In all there were seven of us, but only four had the courage to fish for the carp. I had booked the Parlour Pool for the day and around nine o'clock I missed a cracking bite, with the rod nearly getting pulled off the rests! How it is possible to miss takes like this beggars belief – but miss it I did. However, an hour later I hooked another carp, this time a 13lb common. Again, the Esterberry boilies did the trick. I was beginning to wonder how many carp were in the Parlour Pool stretch or were moving in and out during the day, because whenever I cast a boilie in I was getting takes.

You must remember that all this was going on in the middle of winter and hardly anyone had bothered to seriously carp fish the Royalty during the colder months. Two of the other lads came along to see me just after the common had been returned and asked if I would mind them fishing above me in the Parlour stretch. I did not mind because it was a social day out and I wanted everyone to catch.

They returned to the tackle shop and exchanged their tickets for Parlour tickets (it costs a little more) and set up just below the sluice gates. Around four o' clock, Andy Skinner recast a lump of luncheon meat towards the far bank and it was taken before it hit the bottom. A twenty-minute battle ensued, with the fish going all over the top of the pool before it was netted. We had seen that it was a mirror during the fight, and that it was at least 20lb, but we were not prepared for a new Royalty record of 30lb 4oz!

By now nothing surprised me about the Royalty. I do have to admit I was just a little jealous of Andy, but surely that is human nature.

During the winter months I had several conversations over the phone with Colin Davidson of *Angler's Mail*. I had sent him the photos of the commons that I'd caught, and after he'd received the pictures of the thirty-pounder from Andy Sloane he

The author with a beautiful 17lb 12oz common from the River Avon

phoned to ask if I fancied going down to the Royalty with him. Well, by now I was so keen to fish the Avon as much as I could I'd have taken the wife down there for the day. A date was set and I phoned Davis Angling to see if I could book the Parlour for myself and Colin. The date we wanted was free so all was set.

Colin stayed with me the night before and we left the house at 4.30am for the two-hour drive to Hampshire. I was a little concerned because I had spoken to Andy the previous night and he told me that the river had fined down and lost a lot of the colour it had been carrying so far that winter. Andy himself had spent a rare day's fishing and had not seen a carp in the Parlour Pool all day. Having told Colin how good the fishing had been I was worried that we might suffer a blank day. I needn't have worried.

It was much more relaxing knowing that the pool was already booked and that we wouldn't have to worry about other anglers beating us to the better swims. As we stood on the parapet above the sluice gates I explained to Colin where all my fish had been caught, and being a gentleman I even gave him the choice of swims. He preferred the look of the bottom end of the pool where there were some overhanging trees which the carp seemed to like lying under. That was also good news for me because I wanted to fish the top end where the big mirror had been caught.

It took me all of five minutes to get my baits out. Colin took a little longer but it was only just after eight o'clock when I looked up to see him playing a fish. I quickly wound my rods in and went down to give him a hand landing it. Like most people, the power of the carp surprised him as it battled away in the steady flow, but we had seen it several times in the clear water and he was convinced that it was a low double. I kept quiet about this because from the other carp I had caught I knew that these Avon carp were very solidly built and had been caught out by their weight before. I had to get into the water to net it, and as soon as I lifted the net I knew that Colin was going to be surprised by the weight. It proved to be over 18lb. Colin had been instructed to phone his boss Roy Westwood if he caught anything of a reasonable size, and Roy would come along and do the pictures, so the fish was safely sacked in the margins and the mobile phone came out. I returned to my rods and carried on fishing, very relieved that Colin had caught. Now all we needed was for me to get one.

Before too long Roy arrived and the pictures were taken. Just seconds after the carp had been released Colin had another bite and landed another carp of 14lb. After all this excitement I returned to my swim and began fishing again. Before too long I had two or three hefty bangs on the rod tips and I felt sure that I would get a take any minute. In fact, the rod tip kept knocking for nearly half an hour before I got a take. I shouted to the others who were still talking at the other end of the pool and they came along to help. I saw the carp early in the fight and once again it was a common. This one fought as though its life depended on it. It must have been fifteen minutes before Colin netted it for me, during which time Roy shot a roll of film of me playing the carp. I had not beaten Colin's first fish, but at 17lb 10oz I was chuffed. All this action came within the first ninety minutes of starting, and once again the rest of the day was blank, except for a chub that Colin caught on a bunch of lobworms.

It was becoming apparent that if you were going to get some action it was going to come in very short bursts and the rest of the time it would be deadly quiet. There didn't seem to be a favourite time for takes; they would come at any time, but you could not expect to get takes all day long. This may have been because the feeding times were only very short and could start at any point during the day, or that the carp moved in and out of the Parlour in small shoals. You would get a take from them as they came by, but by catching you would spook the rest of the shoal. I still have no real idea, but Andy is convinced it has to do with the effects of the tides on the river, and having worked on the river for ten years he has had plenty of time to formulate his ideas. I for one am not going to argue with him on the subject and I always listen keenly when he is giving advice on where to fish.

By this stage I'd had four trips, caught four fish and lost another two and the season was drawing to a close. Weekend trips were out of the question because of the family, and like most others I have a full-time job, albeit on a self-employed basis, so I did not know if I would be able to go again. But as the temperatures dropped dramatically it became too cold for me to work, so my partner and I shot down mid-week. I was not

confident of catching because the three previous nights it had reached −5° Centigrade and we had also had snow, but with time running out I wanted to get down there as much as possible.

Arriving at 7am we were first in the queue outside the tackle shop; in fact, we were the only two outside the tackle shop. I was hoping that, being mid-week, nobody would have booked the Parlour and that Tony and I would be able to book it for the day. Luckily the Parlour was free, so we paid our money and off we went. Once again I wanted Tony to catch so I advised him to fish where Colin had stood under the trees, whilst I again fished the head of the pool. During the morning Tony had a couple of drop backs but failed to connect with anything. Up the top of the pool all was still. All morning I watched the tips, but however hard I tried I could not make them move. By dinnertime I decided that I would move below Tony to the very end of the Parlour stretch by the boundary fence. Both baits were cast to the far margin and twenty baits thrown around each. By now the day had warmed up and I sat on the chair almost nodding off. Tony's buzzer woke me as his bobbin dropped a couple of inches but refused to do any more; probably a chub I told him.

By mid-afternoon I was seriously questioning my judgement in driving all that way for a day's fishing, when the right-hand rod tip bounced viciously and the rod nearly leapt from the rests. With my chair set up right next to the rods I was able to grab it quickly as a very angry carp headed for the fast water at the bottom of the pool. There was another angler below me fishing Watersmeet but he quickly saw what was happening and wound his rod in as the carp powered through his swim. With heavy side strain I managed to stop the carp, but it then headed into the nearside margin which caused me a problem because there was a fence sticking into the water. Luckily my

The other side of the typical unmarked Avon common shown on page 29.

rods are thirteen-footers and the extra length and long arms helped me keep the line out of the fence. Eventually the fish came upstream, and above me we could see it spinning in the water trying to shed the hook, then diving down out of sight. Once again the extending handle of the landing net saved us the problem of getting the fish through the weed in the margin.

When Tony saw it in the bottom of the net his description of it was unprintable, but as usual it was immaculate and the body was solid. It weighed 21lb 12oz, my second twenty of the winter on the Avon on only my fifth trip. The Royalty was amazing that winter; in total I fished for seven days and caught five fish, losing two. My last two trips in February were both blanks; on the first one I didn't have a bite, but on the second I had two takes in two minutes. The first one shed the hook but the second one broke the hook link on the strike. The bubble had burst as far my luck was concerned, but what a winter's fishing. Two twenty-pounders from a river in winter can't be bad; in fact I thought it was brilliant – well worth all the travelling and all the early morning starts.

As you can see, I only fished a small part of the river so there are probably more hotspots to be found, but all the time I was catching I was not going to move off them!

4 The Bristol Avon Record

Adam Scott

The known population of carp in this stretch of the Avon is small, possibly as few as a dozen fish. The carp found their way down the river after a local trout farm closed, emptying their renegade carp into the nearest river. Most local anglers, even non-carp anglers, knew that the carp were in the area. But time had passed, the carp had grown, and most people had forgotten. Not I!

This particular year my normal routine of two days and two nights per week was about to change due to a redirection of my career. Most of the next six months would be spent trudging round the mountains of Wales, carrying my house on my back. So with limited time on my hands I needed a challenge close to home that would provide a big fish for the album.

During a visit to the local tackle shop, the owner mentioned a big fish in the nearby river that caught my attention. The fish was apparently seen by a warm water outlet which flows from the spa town (there's a clue) into the river in the grounds of the city centre park.

Initially, I played down my interest and changed the subject. But after leaving the shop with my compulsory brown paper bag costing £30, I rushed down to the hot springs. Looking over the railings into three feet of clear water I could see a huge shoal of small fry diving into the current along with an occasional chub.

I looked hard, trying to see through the thick shoal of 'rudd scales', and after a minute or so my eyes adjusted to this confusing spectacle. I began to make out the occasional shape moving deep down on the bottom. They were definitely carp – only a couple – but they were not the monsters I'd expected.

Several more trips down to the hot springs followed, at this stage only in an attempt to spy the residents and find out what their habits were. I would often find two or three fish feeding on natural food right at the base of the underwater pipe. I could see particles of food or weed being blown through this pipe so they may have been grazing on this. Breadflake was accepted enthusiastically, but the chub were far faster off the mark and nailed nine out of ten pieces I threw in.

One evening after the park rangers had left, I hopped over the wall and walked down to the railings. Taking care to keep my shadow off the water I peeked over the edge and saw the usual two or three carp. One fish looked to be a low twenty mirror, one a low twenty common, and one a low double linear. The linear often gave away its presence by head and shouldering or sending up three or four large bubbles. After half an hour I relaxed and became a little more casual with my movements. I stood up straight and moved slightly. There was a small movement to my right and a grey ghostly shape edged towards the pack of three. This was definitely the carp I'd been looking for. It looked to be at least 33lb, very short, but with a distinctive thick wrist to its tail. This big fish behaved in a completely different way to the others. It often swam mid-water and was extremely edgy in its movements. It knew I was there I'm sure, and soon left, moving slowly downstream.

My first success at the river was a strange affair in as much as my girlfriend Gill actually found the carp for me. Let me explain. I would often take Gill to the hot springs where she would be employed keeping the ducks occupied downstream, whilst I fed the carp in the overflow pipe. She fed bread to the ducks, whilst I fed all manner of tasty things to the odd carp. Whilst I concentrated on the carp's reactions, Gill called out that there was a 'big one' eating her bread. Thinking that it was probably a chub I ambled over only to find a large common carp literally chasing the ducks for the bread. I reckoned this fish weighed a little over 20lb so it more than interested me.

That evening I waited at the park gates until the rangers had gone, then crept down to the railings and tossed in a couple of bread crusts. I immediately saw a carp rise slowly and take the bread. This was too good an opportunity to miss, so I plonked the hook-bait right into the middle of the disturbance. Up came the carp and down went the bread, so I jerked up the rod top to set the hook. I expected the fish to tear off up the margins – after all, river carp are supposed to really fight – but it just wallowed on the surface. I leant over the railings and scooped it up, the whole procedure lasting no more than twenty seconds. I weighed the fish – it was the common, by the way – at just under 19lb. The fish was easily big enough to weigh twenty plus but seemed very hollow.

By that point I believed that the best way to single out this lone big mirror was to catch it off the top. That way I could be sure that I would not have the bait nabbed by the smaller carp, or worse the dreaded chub.

A couple more sessions ended in the capture of another common of 13lb – and I also hooked a linear which I lost at the net. Although it was only about 6lb, it put up by far the hardest fight of the fish so far hooked.

At the same time a few other anglers were starting to fish for the carp, but they were fishing from the far bank and casting across. I was fairly sure that the big fish would not put up with the noise of a lead whacking down in three foot of water. Far better to sneak down for an hour or two under cover of darkness and go about my task in secrecy…

I never managed to find the big mirror feeding on the surface, and I was getting more than a little concerned that whilst hooking the other fish I might have spooked the big mirror from the area.

The next visit saw me putting in small handfuls of tiger nuts, but only when the carp were there. I could not risk getting chubbed out on the tigers. The carp showed immediate interest, up-ending in the current and competing for every item.

I baited the overflow once more before fishing it. Using float tackle I quickly hooked a powerful fish which stripped yards and yards from the spool. I was convinced this was the big mirror, although because it was almost dark I couldn't be sure. The fight became all the more nerve-wracking because I knew the river was quite snaggy in this area. The commotion caused by me hooking, playing and eventually landing this fish had drawn quite a crowd.

I hauled the net over the railings and quickly realized that this was not the big mirror. Nevertheless, I was pleased with this low twenty mirror.

After I had returned the fish, a couple of Japanese tourists who had been watching the fight from a platform above the water said the fish I had hooked was followed through some of the fight by a much bigger fish. It must have been the big mirror, and I prayed it had not been spooked by the event.

I baited the swim several times during the following week. Each time I saw the big mirror, and each time it looked so confident eating the bait. I could now get a much bet-

Adam Scott with the Bristol Avon record 31lb mirror.

ter idea of its weight, which I put at about 32lb.

All my efforts would now be rewarded. The waiting for the park rangers to leave, the walking to and from the river, the hassle from the chub, and the trouble from the local drunks would all be worth it if I caught this fish.

I arrived early at about 7pm and jumped over the wall to the park. I tackled up the rod, set up the net, and threaded the tiger nuts on to the hair. I baited the hot springs overflow and awaited the arrival of the mirror. Within minutes it was on the spot, tail waving in the boiling current. I lowered the float down beside the fish and watched for

35

over a minute whilst the float was jostled by the carp. As with the bites I'd had before, the float just disappeared leaving a stream of bubbles in its wake. I struck and hung on for grim death as the fish tore off over forty yards of line. It only stopped when it got to the far bank, where it kited downstream using the current to aid its progress. My little ten-foot Avon rod was bent past the handle. The reel swivelled within the fittings so I gripped tighter and continued the battle. I took my time coaxing the fish to the net, but the runs gradually became shorter and eventually I must have bundled it into the net. By then everything was blurred in the excitement.

After hoisting the mirror over the railings, I laid it on the wet grass and checked the hook-hold. The flyliner hook was lodged at least three inches back into its mouth; so far, in fact, that I needed my homemade lollypop stick disgorger to nudge the hook out!

I weighed the fish carefully as I knew it would be the river record, and at 31lb exactly it was just that. As far as I know, the fish had never been caught before and it has never been caught since.

5 The Lincolnshire Fens

Gary Dennis

The midday sun beat down, burning my bare shoulders. Just for once we were experiencing a summer in Lincolnshire, and rather than creeping around a deserted carp water trying to tempt one of its inhabitants with a floating bait, I was cutting cauliflowers; sweating and burning, the thought of an ice-cold lager sliding down my arid, dry throat was becoming unbearable.

Coming to the end of the field, we found ourselves on the banks of one of the Fens' many drains. The other lads took a well-earned breather whilst I, the only angler in the gang, scanned the featureless, straight stretch of water. Might be worth piking in the winter, I thought to myself. As I looked up and down the drain I noticed the odd, small cluster of reeds and very small lily patches, but otherwise I could see no other weeds. As it was mid-May, other weeds, if present, should have been showing. The water itself was perfectly clear and reflected the blue sky, but it appeared lifeless. Nothing moved at all, flat calm due to the breathless air. So why did the lilies below me rock gently every now and then?

As I watched, something was moving slowly in and around the pads. I eased myself carefully down the steep bank to get a better look and was surprised by what I saw: a common carp around 15lb.

The rest of the day dragged on and on, the heat unbearable, but the sight of that carp had set my mind reeling. I just had to get back to see what else the drain could surprise me with. And get back I did, late afternoon, armed with polarized glasses and a bag of floaters. I spent the rest of the after-noon and evening walking up and down the perfectly straight length of the drain, examining reeds, lilies, the few overhanging bushes and any other likely looking spots hoping to spot a few more carp, which I did. What gorgeous fish! All commons, ranging from 8lb or so up to 20lb or just over.

Corny as it sounds, the fish appeared to lack any caution and just seemed happy to be alive. The drain was crystal clear and its depth was also uniform: three feet for its entire length. The only coloured area I found was a shoal of bream rooting for food in the muddy bottom. A few small roach and one pike (easily over 20lb as well) were the only other fish I saw on that first visit. One thing was absolutely certain though: when the new season opened, I would be fishing here.

To cut a long story short, that weekend I fished a local day ticket water with a friend, and was lucky enough to bank the lake's largest resident. On capture, about thirty people crowded round me and one angler really made my day by announcing that the fish was easy to catch, would weigh 21lb and some ounces, and even revealed its name. It was 21lb 2oz!

'Ian, I need a change from all this and I think I just might have found it,' I said to my friend.

We returned to my home and over coffee I told Ian about my 'find', thinking his eyes would light up with excitement and he would be as keen as me to have a go at the drain. I would just like to say here and now that I shall not be revealing the drain's name, as to this day it is totally neglected, unspoilt and beautiful, and the carp are in no way pressured. They are not in any way easy to catch, but they are not uncatchable. Two very good friends of mine fished there the year before me and kept it to themselves, but when we became a bit of a team they asked me to keep quiet, so out of respect for a beautiful, unspoilt water and friendship, the name remains with me. It is south of my Skegness home is all I will say!

When I had finished raving on, Ian merely smiled into his coffee. In his living room he has a framed photograph of an unusual 25lb mirror; unusual in the way that its head and about one third of its body on its right-hand side are white, with the rest being a lovely deep purple on top, tapering down to an orange belly. A rush of excitement raced through my body when he (at last) revealed where he had caught it. It was from the lower part of the drain. We talked until late and Ian told me of his sessions on the drain. He had not put in a lot of time, as it was almost autumn when he started fishing there and his love of pike pulled him away from the carp for the year. But as well as the two-tone twenty, he had had a few other fish, all commons, all doubles up to 18lb.

We decided to fish seriously on the drain that coming season, and also decided to make a few examination trips to try to learn more, find an area each and bait it ready for midnight on 15 June. On each trip we saw carp; again, all were double-figure fish and all were commons. What the carp did not reveal to us was if they preferred one area to another. They just seemed to be evenly spread throughout the entire length in groups of two, three or four. A slight preference to any reed or pad was all we could agree upon, but then, all carp love a feature.

After much searching we found two swims for the start. We decided on this particular stretch for a number of reasons, such as Ian's success in one swim, the nice patches of reeds and pads to fish to, and the fact that it was well out of the way, as for some of the length a road runs directly behind the swims. A very rough track led to our area and we could fish from the car so to speak, parking directly behind the swims we chose.

Bait was the next item to be discussed. Obviously we wanted something we knew to be reliable and effective, but also felt that the fish were not too clued up as to bait. The only anglers on the drain were match anglers, and we joked that we should use maggots and hemp, but as it turned out we did use hemp as a feed to fish over. Ian used baits made from Mainline's Grange base mix, whilst I decided that my usual bait would be perfect. Martin Locke's excellent Solar range of baits and tackle has always proved very successful for me, so I stuck with my Neptune base mix, with squid and octopus koi rearer as the flavour. These were rolled to 18mm and the hook-baits would be fished as pop-ups due to a light covering of silkweed on the bottom in places. I had to know my hook-baits would be fishing as near perfect as possible, so pop-ups were a very safe bet.

The prebaiting began at the start of June and took place three evenings a week at the time we would usually be setting up for our overnight sessions. My swim was and still is the most beautiful spot on earth. The drain's width doesn't really alter anywhere along its length, being roughly fifty to sixty feet wide, and on both banks the sides are built up with corrugated sheets of asbestos. Over the years the sheets have become overgrown, although the grass has not yet reached the surface of the water. Opposite the swim two or three willows reach down to the water – a lovely sight.

My right-hand rod was to be cast down slightly to the right, to a very small patch of reeds tight to the side. The left rod was to be fished up against a patch of lilies slightly to the left. Ian's swim was very similar but he decided upon three rods with one rod mid-stream.

Gary Dennis with a typical Fens common.

Each time we went to prebait we saw fish. Again, they were all over the place, so our bait was not holding them to the one area. Incidentally, we used the same prebait as we intended using on opening night: two pounds of hemp per rod and thirty boilies per rod.

June the fifteenth dragged at work – I mean really dragged! The last three days had been cold and wet but the fifteenth was hot, still and sunny, so naturally I was itching to get off the cauli field and to the drain, this time to fish. I had arranged to meet Ian at the swims around six o'clock, but I was there at four! Funny thing was, Ian was there half an hour after me, just as full of confidence.

The first job was to bait our areas with the usual amounts. We then set up our rods and all the other items. So neglected and over-grown is the drain that to ensure the long grass didn't snag the swinger indicators or

the line, I used a rod mat to flatten it down slightly. I also knew that the grass would soon spring back upright when I removed the mat. Everything made ready, I placed the bedchair next to the rods and sat back to survey the scene. God, it looked and felt good! Roll on midnight. I fetched a fish and chip tea and a couple of lagers, and as we both ate, a bow wave gently pushed along the far side over my bait. Where to take the photographs seemed to be my only worry.

Midnight eventually arrived and both rods were cast across to the chosen areas, both with 18mm pop-ups, 12in-long braided hook lengths and 2oz in-line leads. A couple of pouchfuls of hemp, ten more boilies, and then it was up to the carp. All was silent but excitement made me very restless and I could not get comfortable on the bedchair. In a bush by my side a nightingale started to sing – and didn't pause, even to draw breath, until dawn. I am a nature

39

lover but that bloody bird drove me mad! By two o'clock I could not believe that I had not had a fish. I was unable to doze off even though I had been up since four o'clock the previous morning and had worked hard all day. It was extremely hot and by now I was bunged-up with hayfever, not to mention that damn bird! I was not a happy chap.

Around 3.30am I heard panting and running feet coming towards me on the gravel track to my rear.

'Bloody hell Gaz, how many have you had?' asked Ian, collapsing on to the grass.

'Not a bloody bleep,' I replied, and added my tale of woe.

'Oh, well, I, erm, I've had three and lost one.'

'Yeah? Good fish Ian?' I asked, a tad jealous.

'A12lb 2oz, 14lb 2oz and 16lb 11oz in that order.'

I walked back with him to take photos before the float lads arrived, and if I said they were gorgeous fish in the water, they were something else on the bank: absolutely immaculate, never-before-caught commons. As long as I live I will never forget those fish in the semi-light of that opening day dawn. We packed away around six o'clock and drove to Ian's house for a cooked breakfast and then spent opening day fishing a small river for chub, our aim a four-pounder, but we were more than happy with the threes we landed.

When we had left the drain it was filling up with float anglers, but when we returned to the same swims that teatime it was deserted. Tiredness was catching up with us so we set up the rods and cast out, then pulled the umbrella down low and fell asleep. Awaking to a cup of tea was very nice and I felt much better, but as Ian pointed out, darkness was not far away so I recast, rebaited and made ready for the night.

I had just finished all this when I heard Ian's buzzer cry out – he was into a fish again. As I knelt with the net I was stunned by the speed of the fish. I was convinced it was a biggie, such was its power and the length of time it took to subdue it. It weighed 2oz short of 14lb, was again a common, and was absolutely perfect in every way. It seemed a shame to put a hook in such a fantastic creature. What also shocked me was Ian's claim that this fish had fought poorly in comparison to the others.

As the fish quietly slid away from Ian's hands, another buzzer split the evening air. At last, it was one of mine. In a moment I was with my rods and saw the right-hand rod being almost wrenched from the rests, such was the speed of the take. I dropped the bail arm in and instantly the rod was pulled flat and the clutch shrieked in pain.

A typical drain in the Lincolnshire Fens.

A bow wave was flying down the far side of the drain and was determined not to come back to where it had been hooked. I'd never hooked such a crazy fish; it almost seemed to destroy the drain, smashing up a small lily patch, rooting reeds and clumps of silkweed. I announced to Ian that this was huge, a serious carp. He just laughed and said, 'Welcome to drain carp.' When eventually landed, the fish weighed 11lb 4oz. Eleven four! What on earth would a twenty feel like, or a carp from a river with a strong flow?

Incidentally, the drain always seemed unmoving to the glance, but a closer inspection would show a very, very slight movement (even in no wind) towards the sea.

So I'd opened my account. We noted that the fish was very light coloured; all the others were quite dark. I had a second take on the same rod at 6.30 the next morning which produced a lovely 13lb 3oz fish. It also fought like a demon and was flawless, totally unmarked. With the very odd exception, all the fish we had went berserk and fought like nothing else I've ever hooked. I don't want to bore you with a long drawn-out description of every fight, but they certainly go!

That was opening night and I counted it as a success. Seven takes between us and only one lost, which Ian said was on, then off.

I next managed a session on 22 June. My work dictates much of what I do, and fishing often suffers, but creeping around bosses, swapping jobs around, or a day off for the gang usually led to me having a session when I felt conditions were right or I just simply needed to be there. To fish and then go to work would mean packing away at 3.30am at the latest to get to our fields on time. Not good. Anyway, the gang was off on the 22nd so I left around 6pm the day before, relaxed in the knowledge that I had the next day to do as I pleased. I spent a couple of hours riding up and down search-ing for signs of fish but never saw a thing. The weather was still and muggy and I eventually set up in the swim I had first fished. It looked good, as it always does, but I never saw a ripple from a carp, and pulling the sleeping bag over me around midnight I was not confident, even mulling over in my mind a water to shoot off to the following day.

At 2am I had the usual ripping take on the left rod cast to the lilies. I was able to follow the fish's movements easily, as the night was now flooded with light from the full moon. It turned out to be the smallest fish I ever took from the drain, and weighed 8lb 4oz. I was away shortly after 5am due to the noise of float anglers and the number of people quizzing me as to what I was fishing for.

'Eels mate,' was the usual reply, either meeting with laughter or a barrage of questions as to why I should want to catch horrible, slimy eels!

I returned that night to fish with Ian, but the weather had turned wet, windy and cool in a matter of a few hours during the day and we both blanked. I was away again at 5am, this time to attend my cousin's wedding in Luton. This was also the session, my diary shows, during which the eels took a liking to squid and octopus flavour and I was up all night striking flying takes that only produced chewed baits and tangled hook lengths covered in snot! Time to alter the bait, I thought.

The new bait was one I'd fancied for a while and again came from Solar. I used the Dairy Cream base mix and added Ester-blend 12 liquid flavour and a blueberry flavour which was in powder form and smelt absolutely gorgeous. I obtained this powder when I worked for Rod Hutchinson, but it was never sold to the public. I coloured the bait orange and knew immediately it would catch, so returned to my swim on the drain on Monday 26 June.

From the moment I arrived I saw fish and expected quite a catch, but I was not disappointed with a 14lb fish at 5.30am, just as I was preparing to pack away. So the new bait worked, but I think any bait put together and presented correctly would catch. I did make one mistake though, and that was the bait's colour. As soon as it got light, the coots loved it on the left-hand rod but never touched the right-hand bait, whilst the fish took the right-hand bait. Funny eh?

Tuesday night I was there again. The weed covering the bottom of the drain was causing a few problems, so I increased the hook lengths to 18in and PVA'd a cork to the hook before casting. This ensured that when the PVA melted, the pop-up only just floated down to rest on the weed or clear bottom if the cast was spot on. The evening was breezy and sunny but by dusk heavy cloud had rolled in and a light rain was falling. At five minutes to three, the right-hand rod trundled off very slowly. The fish did not fight at all and initially I thought it was a bream, but the small torch revealed a very strangely shaped fish of 10lb 4oz. At dawn the whole swim was a mass of bubbles rising to the surface but no further action occurred. I think they were bream.

Friday 30 June produced a blank session for me but an eight-pounder for Ian. I knew nothing about it as tiredness had caught up with me after a busy week and the evening was grey and cool, so I just dived into the bag under the umbrella at about 10 o'clock. Very bad angling, I know!

The following Friday, Ian and I decided upon a new area two miles upstream, as he'd been for a walkabout during the week and had seen some very good fish. He said two fish cruised under his nose, both well over 20lb, and just hung around the area all evening. This particular area was quite different to our previous spots, having the road directly behind the drain. Both banks were very steep and the only swims were gaps in the bushes. The opposite bank was also dense with large thorn bushes and lilybeds

of quite a size spread along the length. It looked very good indeed.

Whilst I tackled-up, I noticed a pike under the rod tips which was easily an upper double. As I watched, it was joined by a lighter coloured fish; but what a fish. It was immense, easily mid-twenties, and together they slowly cruised off. Needless to say I virtually beat the water to a froth with various lures, but I never even had a follow. Back to the carp and again a very big fish at my feet, only this time I had a baited rod in my hand! I very slowly lowered the bait just in front of the common, and as it touched bottom the fish shot forward, sucked in the bait, spat it out and bolted away, pushing a huge bow wave in front of it. Ian thought I'd hooked a fish, such was the disturbance of the water's surface.

I was gobsmacked! My faith in line aligners was somewhat dented, such was the ease with which the carp ejected the bait. All night long, carp bow waved and swirled in the stretch, but the only action was a ripping take for Ian at around 3am, which on striking met thin air. Perhaps the fish were cuter than we thought!

The cauli-cutting season was by now in full swing, with some serious money to be earned, and it wasn't until 12 July that I got back to the bush length, or at least that's where I ended up. I actually got to the drain at 6pm, but such was my keenness to catch a fish and with only an evening session possible, I spent too long looking for fish and it was 8pm before I cast out. As I was packing away at 10.30pm, with eight swans directly over the left-hand bait, I had a take on this rod. It was a very hard fight, which resulted in the tip ring becoming bunged with silk weed, and finally ended with an eleven-pounder being handlined into the net. It was also the only time I had another angler witness any of my fish, but he turned out to be very helpful in a time of need.

The weather had been very still and hot for days, and this evening was no different.

Due to the bottom weed, finding clear spots was becoming quite difficult and the thought of using neutral buoyancy baits was in my mind.

Ian and I fished Friday night as usual but the weather was horrible – it was raining and the wind was blowing downstream, uprooting the snot weed and making it clog up the lines. We did, however, see fish gliding around beneath the waves but received no action. I was also using beds of moth beans as I'd run out of hemp.

Sunday afternoon was back to blistering heat with a now gentle breeze. I hadn't had one on floater as yet and it seemed a good chance to rectify that. I didn't catch on floater but I did catch my largest drain carp in the middle of the afternoon, proving Ian's original theory of night-time action only totally wrong.

Ian was wandering up and down when I arrived about 1 o'clock but had yet to cast as the only fish showing were cruising along the bottom, occasionally drifting into the pads. From the top of the high bank I scanned the area and saw that where I'd baited with moth beans on the Friday night was totally cleared out, and instead of silkweed the bottom was clear! I rebaited this spot and cast a pop-up on top, then put the right-hand rod downstream to a patch of reeds with a pop-up directly off the lead, on a six-inch link. I put no free offerings around this rod. Fish continued to drift aimlessly around the pads and over the baits but not one stopped to feed. By four o'clock the sun had disappeared and so had my fingernails! Surely one would make a mistake? And it did! I never even knew the fish was over the bait as I hadn't seen a single ripple or shadow for fifteen minutes or so, but suddenly the water exploded and the buzzer screamed. The fish fought slower than any other fish, but for much longer, and I was greatly relieved that the fish went into the net when it did as my arms were killing me. It was obviously larger than any other fish

I'd taken but had a very hollow belly. It weighed exactly 18lb, but with a full stomach we guessed it would have been just over 20lb. Fish were still showing so I recast until ten o'clock but received no further action.

I was very pleased with the eighteen-pounder but felt a larger fish could still end up on the bank. Sadly, due to work the only trips I managed were fish-spotting ones. Twice I found a group of fish milling around in a fairly barren area; there were no bushes on either bank and the only underwater features were odd reed stems here and there and quite a large bed of Canadian pondweed. The water increased in depth slightly for about 200 yards, then dropped to four feet. I called this area 'Yellow Flowers', as opposite the patch of Canadian weed was a patch of, well, yellow flowers! I fished this new area on 24 July for an evening and took an 11lb 4oz fish at 7.30pm, another daylight fish that took a double pop-up over hemp, and was fished up against four reed stems tight to the boarding. It was a lovely evening but it was the only fish I saw.

I think everyone has a session from time to time that can only be described as an utter disaster. Well, the following was my disaster session of the year.

I pulled off the road and on to the grass verge at the sight of two bow waves and went to investigate. This was where I'd caught the eighteen, and yes, two fish were moving upstream with their backs out of the water, both low doubles. They were moving without stopping to 'browse', and after standing watching for half an hour I knew they would not stay in the area. I saw nothing more. I jumped back in my Escort XR3 and turned the key. The car turned over but failed to fire up. I tried everything that I knew, which I must admit is minimal, but the car would not start and the battery was becoming weak. For once, the road was deserted so there was no one to lend a hand.

Suddenly, I noticed just how remote the

Gary Dennis with a Lincolnshire Fens 16lb 10oz common.

Lincolnshire Fens were. Usually we were trying to hide the fact that we were pursuing (and catching) carp. There was one last saviour: my mobile phone. Or rather there wasn't; I'd put it on charge when I returned home from work and had forgotten it. Damn! I walked back into the swim to think about the situation. No way was I leaving my car with all my gear in it whilst I walked to a house or phone box, as the nearest was about four miles away.

A carp swam past my feet, turned and crossed the drain, and bubbled its head off under the lily pads. Great. This problem and a swim full of feeding fish. I decided to cast the rods out and sit at the top of the bank, hoping to stop a car. If I didn't get to

work the next morning there would be hell to pay. Anyway, someone eventually stopped and he was a mechanic. What I'd done was pull the wires off the fuel pump as I'd driven through the long grass, the pump being situated underneath the car at the rear end. Just to be safe I wound in and drove home, not a happy chappy!

My return was the final day of July and produced a good fish, but not a carp unfortunately. More fun and games here! The silkweed in Yellow Flowers was very thick, so some casting around for clear spots was needed, and I was doing this with a lead and hook length when I became attached to something heavy that was moving. At first I thought I'd foul hooked a big bream due to the slow pull, but the fish that surfaced after a few minutes was no bream – it was a bloody great pike. It weighed 17lb and was hooked inside the mouth, all fair and square, but why it grabbed a black hook I'll never know. I took a quick photo then watched her glide away again – only to see her come belly-up in the centre of the drain. I stood unable to reach the fish for a moment or two, then I jumped straight in, waded across to the fish and scooped it into my arms.

The well-being of any fish is most important to me, and this beautiful pike was no exception. No way was this fish going to die. It took just over an hour to fully revive the fish, but I did it and she eventually swam away, this time staying down. The night produced no carp, but I did see a shoal of tench feeding when I got up at dawn to answer nature's calling!

Work commitments reared again, and a holiday fishing for catfish kept me away from the drain until 25 August. The water level had dropped by some eighteen inches and for this reason I set up in the slightly deeper Yellow Flowers section. Twenty minutes to midnight produced a fish of 11lb 9oz – my last of the year from the drain. What with less light in the evenings, low water levels and pike, Ian and I went off to throw deadbaits around. Does the drain produce carp in winter? I don't know as we've never fished later than early September. I doubt it, due to the low water, but where they go in the colder months no one seems to know; possibly into another drain as our drain joins another, or into the town that the drain flows through. There is just so much water to explore in the future, but what I have experienced so far is all down here.

My second summer on the drain was cut short due to having my right leg smashed in four places, so I'll try to cover the few things that happened. Ian and I baited our previous season's spots for ten days prior to opening night. I still used the Dairy Cream base mix with squid and octopus and Esterblend 12. Partiblend was the feed this year. After setting up I popped to the town to fetch fish and chips and a lager each to toast the new season. On our arrival we had seen fish, and strangely they were all heading downstream. Neither of us had a single bleep all night, and driving around next morning it was obvious where they were all heading. They were stacked up in a bay-like lagoon and they were spawning! That was opening night.

I returned three days later and immediately my feelings were of sadness and anger. Two weed-cutting boats had decimated the whole length of the drain. Not a reed or lily remained, and one of the boats was leaking either oil or diesel into the water. I also found a pike of around 8lb with a huge gash in its side. I was heartbroken; my paradise was ruined. I phoned Ian with the news and he said it would all grow back soon and wasn't too worried, but I couldn't stay. I just threw the phone into the car and drove away.

Ian phoned a week later to tell me that the lilies were already showing again. I got the gear together and shot off the next evening for a night session. I was very pleased when I arrived at my opening night swim and saw the left-hand lilybed had reappeared, although it was somewhat thinned out. The weather was sunny and very warm with a light downstream breeze, and in the first hour I saw four good fish, one of them a mirror, which was very unusual, but not *the* mirror!

I had fish at 2.15am and 5.15am, one on each rod. The first fish was 11lb 12oz, and the second 12lb 11oz. As I was taking photographs a float angler pulled up and saw me with the fish. He'd been smashed up many times by the carp but had never seen one landed. He also promised to say nothing.

And that's where the story ends really, because one week later I managed to trap my right leg under a two-ton forklift and broke my ankle and foot in four places. I spent the rest of the summer in plaster cast and was unable to do anything really, let alone go fishing. I was very, very miserable.

Looking back through my diary on this cold, wet November night, I can easily remember those sessions. The smell of the lightly rippled clear water with dark-backed commons sliding through the weeds, the birdsong on a still evening, the sight of a gorgeous carp laying on the unhooking mat surrounded by wild, damp flowers and grass – it was just fantastic. I also remember the planning, the searching for fish, casting for clear spots, altering rigs to combat the silkweed, trying to decide which swim those bow waves would cease in and the fish would start to sniff around for food in.

Ian was great company and a very good angler who sorted out many a problem. He had less time available to him than I had but enjoyed every minute he fished. To some people, my largest drain fish of 18lb would mean nothing – not big enough. To me, it was equal to a southern-gravel-pit thirty. Hard work, lots of planning and lots of thinking led to that fish; a Fen drain fish, not a lake fish. To me, those drain fish were worlds apart from lake fish. They behaved differently, they fought differently, they looked different. That was and still is the huge attraction. What they could never do when hooked was swim away or go down. They either went left or right, and they did it at one hell of a speed. You knew that when the fish was in the net, it had fought for its life, literally, because they knew nothing other than survival as they were not regular bank visitors like some lake fish. We never had a recapture other than the mid-twenty mirror which I never caught, although Ian and a friend of his did.

If there is a remote drain near you, spend some time looking for carp. If carp are present, fish for them as I'm sure you will enjoy it. If I hadn't been cutting that one particular field and seen that fish, I wouldn't have experienced the most enjoyable fishing of my life.

6 The River Gipping

Ted Head

Sadly, Ted died late in 1999 before he had a chance to read the book and see his pieces on the River Gipping and Suffolk Stour. He passed away fishing the very swim where, in June 1995, he caught the biggest carp ever landed from a British river. It was, I think, a fitting way for him to go. I will remember him for the picture of him holding that mighty mirror, and I hope every one else will do likewise.

Rest in peace.

During my years fishing for river carp I have often been told that I need my brain tested. On several occasions I've been inclined to agree, however despite this I'm still at it.

Don't let these remarks put you off. River carping is not only fascinating, but very rewarding at times, especially when you pull your first river twenty over the net. But should you feel inclined to give it a try, do not expect to start catching twenty- or thirty-pounders right away because you will be disappointed. I can promise you this, however: when you hook your first river fish, you will be pleasantly surprised as they fight much harder than their stillwater cousins.

Most of our rivers hold carp to some extent, some will hold 20lb fish, with the odd thirty-pounder showing up at times. There are exceptions, however, with much larger fish being taken out of the blue. Nine times out of ten, these fish will be escapees from flooded stillwaters.

In my opinion there are only two, or possibly three rivers in this country which are capable of producing a genuine 40lb carp: the Thames, Trent and the Severn. Years ago some very big lumps were reported from the Nene around Peterborough, but this seems to have gone quiet in recent years.

After twenty-odd years fishing for river carp, I've only managed to take one fish over 30lb, although I've had hundreds of doubles, with numerous twenties up to 27lb. One thing that I have noticed is that a large percentage of the fish are commons. However, in saying this, most of my big twenties have been mirrors.

If you are tempted, one of the first things you must do is to walk the banks of the areas you intend to fish. You will need a good pair of legs as long distances are normally involved. The carp are invariably nomadic, and are hard to find at times, but if you can find them you will catch them. One other important thing is to make a point of talking to any pleasure anglers. They will queue up to tell you about the monster fish hooked and lost last week, and it's a good bet that it was a carp.

Most of my river carping involves two rivers, the River Gipping and the Suffolk Stour, so my findings are based on these venues.

The Gipping is a short river compared to some, around thirty to forty miles from source to estuary, running entirely through Suffolk. In fact it isn't really a river, more of a stream, until it reaches the Stowmarket area. Here it starts to widen and deepen and is capable of holding carp.

I have little knowledge of the river until it reaches the village of Claydon on the outskirts of Ipswich. Carp can be found here on

Ted Head with a mirror of 46½lb from the River Gipping – the British River Record.

Being an industrial area, including a supermarket, the river contains the odd shopping trolley and occasional pushchair. Starting at the railway bridge, for about 800 yards the river is fairly weedy during the summer months, with beds of lilies and so on. The stretch holds a fair head of carp, including a few good twenties. It was from here that I was fortunate enough to catch the existing British River Record in August 1995, a very deep-bodied mirror of 46lb 8oz. It's only fair to mention at this point that this fish did not grow to this size in the river. Dippy, as the fish was named, found its way into the river somehow or other. It's a long story and this fish has quite a long history, but I will make no further comment regarding its background.

Most of the carp in the area were, I understand, introduced to the river by the then National Rivers Authority whilst restocking with batches of small fish of mixed species. This length of river also holds two other large carp, a mirror and a common, which, to date, have never seen the bank; when last seen both looked as big as Dippy.

Being an industrial area, rubbish of all kinds is a problem; there is very little flow and on occasions a condom will drift past in slow motion. If you are lucky it will hang around your line, and if this happens I slacken off. When you get a take the rubber rises out of the water and on the strike it sails up into the air. This puts the fear of Christ up the seagulls!

At the second railway bridge the river gets wider and deepens, holding very little weed with the exception of odd lilybeds. This area is known as Riverside Road and runs through to the Yarmouth Road. During the winter months the carp usually move down to this length from Brook Road. In fact, during the winter of 1995, November to be precise, a friend of mine, Keith Bridges, caught the big mirror at a slightly lower weight – and three-quarters of a mile down-

the Sproughton Lengths, where there is a very good-looking pool. Most of the river in this area is controlled by the local angling club, GAPS. Below here it's mostly private, but one stretch that I managed to fish on a couple of occasions – Fletchers – produced several good doubles with one odd-shaped mirror of just over 20lb.

Downstream from Sproughton the river shallows up, twists and turns, running behind the sugar beet factory until it reaches the railway bridge near the Boss Hall Industrial Estate. This is the area where most of my time has been spent. From here for around one mile the river runs reasonably straight until it reaches what's known as the Yarmouth Road Bridge.

stream from where I had taken it myself in August.

Below the Yarmouth Road the river starts to twist and turn once again. This area is known as West End. Still running through an industrial area it holds a reasonable head of carp – high doubles with the odd twenty. I'm not too familiar with this area, or downstream, so not much information about this I'm afraid.

Tackle-wise I find no need for high-tech gear; as I said earlier, find them and you will catch them. My choice is for 15lb main line, 3oz in-line lead, 9in 15lb clear Amnesia hook length and a size four Drennan Continental Boilie Hook winter and summer. I always fish a popped-up bait. There's no need for small boilies; I usually use double 18mm baits three inches off the bottom during the summer, possibly dropping to a single 18mm bait in the colder months.

During the summer you can usually spot the fish so placing your baits is not a problem, but during the winter it's a different story. Most of the time you will be fishing blind, although the far bank usually has some sort of feature, whether overhanging bushes or beds of brambles. I find the most important feature of all to be beds of reeds, and I usually fish immediately in front of them. You will find clear patches on the bottom and this is where my baits are placed, using either a PVA bag full of trout pellets and a few hook-baits or six-bait stringer. One thing worth mentioning is that because you will be fishing across the flow for most of the time, the majority of takes will show as drop backs, so sitting close to your rods is a must.

Much of the River Gipping is controlled by GAPS, the Gipping Angling Preservation Society. The stretches that hold the big mirror are controlled by the local council and can be fished for a few pounds on day tickets, with no night fishing and two rods only. The bailiff is a chap called Peter Nunn, who carries both season and day tickets.

7 The Suffolk Stour

Ted Head

The Suffolk Stour is a longer river than the Gipping, rising a few miles north of Haverhill and ending at Manningtree where it enters the estuary. Through its entire length there are numerous locks, floodgates and mill pools.

Almost every mill pool holds a few carp, especially during the winter months. In my experience, several of the fish that are found in the pools during winter are fish which have moved upstream, maybe for the deeper water normally associated with these areas. I would think this applies to all rivers, so anyone thinking about giving it a try, don't ignore them; I reckon 90 per cent of my fish are taken from mill pools.

As I mentioned earlier, find them and they can be caught. I don't find it necessary to prebait, in fact I find it detrimental owing to the shoals of bream in the river. These are not small bream either, the majority of the slabs taken accidentally are between 5lb and 9lb. These are either descendants of, or in the case of the bigger fish, originals from several stockings by local clubs from Abberton Reservoir when bream to 16lb were introduced.

Bait-wise it's no different – double 18mm boilies winter and summer. These bream are capable of taking such a big offering with no problem. If possible, I prefer to use a PVA bag filled with trout pellets and a few hook-baits.

Once again, I have very little knowledge of the river until it reaches Clare. Here, it is still very narrow with very little depth, except on some of the many bends. In this particular area, the river runs very close to

the Clare Country Club Lake which holds a number of thirty-pounders. I'm told that during recent floods some of these fish have found their way into the river.

Maybe the best way to describe the river is to name the different stretches along its length, giving the nearest town or village and enlarging on stretches that I'm more familiar with. Downstream from Clare is Glemsford. Here, the river runs close to the LAA pits, which are known to hold carp, but are not seriously fished. There are lots of twists and turns and a fair head of carp reaching high doubles. I suspect that some of these came from the pits.

The next village is Long Melford. Most of the river around here is private, so not much is known. There is, however, one very interesting pool called Liston Mill. This pool stinks of carp. I've not tried it yet, but it has all the characteristics required to hold carp. It is club-controlled by Long Melford AC, as is much of the river in the area.

Further down from Melford is the Rodbridge area. Most of the river here is either controlled by the Sudbury Club or Melford, and holds a good head of carp with the odd 20lb fish showing at times. Near Rodbridge is Borley Mill, well known for its ghosts and mentioned in many books about the supernatural. The pool is private but can be fished on a day ticket if you contact the owner. It's known to hold carp, although I've never fished it myself.

Next from Borley is Kiplings Meadows. This stretch holds a mixture of mirrors and commons, and twists and turns with some good deep bends. My best takes from here

Ted Head with a heavily scaled mirror of 24lb from the Mill Pool on the Suffolk Stour.

are a 24lb mirror and a 21lb common. It is controlled by Sudbury and District AA.

On to Brundon Mill pool. This one holds very special interest for me. I first fished there during the 1960s for pike. At this time I worked for the owner and was lucky enough to gain permission to fish. During one session a small carp was seen to roll. I didn't give it much thought at the time, but about four years ago, when I was fishing the Kiplings and thinking as you do when sitting behind motionless indicators, I remembered this small carp and it dawned on me that it could well be a twenty now. Guess where my next session was going to be!

It is an awkward pool to fish; both banks on the side of the waterfall are private and the only way to fish it is by casting a line from the tail of the pool to the waterfall.

Fairly snaggy with tree stumps sticking out of the water and a large bed of bulrushes to your left, it is a hook and hold situation. There's not a huge head of carp but there are four known twenties and a few high doubles. My best takes from the pool include a common of 24lb and a mirror of 23lb. The common has recently been landed again by Robert Gardiner of Long Melford at exactly the same weight; it seems this fish has no further to go weight-wise. The best fish so far from this pool is a bulky looking mirror of 28lb 2oz, falling to the rods of number two son, Tony.

From Brundon is North Meadows, where the river is fairly straight and flows down to The Croft in Sudbury. It boasts a good head of carp, again with several known twenties and plenty of doubles. This area is part of The Sudbury Common Lands Trust,

51

although it is controlled by Sudbury and District AA. The Trust has some cranky restrictions, for instance no bivvies. My bests from here are a mirror of 25lb and a common of 22lb. As a matter of interest, the mirror had previously been caught by son Tony at 27lb from a pool three-quarters of a mile from where I caught it. Again, it emphasizes the movement of carp from rivers to pools during the winter.

The Croft and Mill Meadows are both part of the Common Lands and the same restrictions apply. In the middle of the two stretches is a small pool known locally as The Floodgates. It looks the part, but never having fished it I couldn't say for certain. There are some good chub though. The river here is all twists and turns with not many carp. The best as far as I know are big doubles. Again, it is controlled by Sudbury and District AA.

Some serious carp inhabit the area by Ballingdon Bridge. By standing on the bridge and looking down into fairly shallow water they can be seen patrolling up and down between beds of lilies. On the mill meadow side of the bridge is a restaurant called The Boathouse, from which day tickets can be purchased. On the other side, both banks are private until the river reaches what's known as The Seven Arches.

Being old and innocent as I am, I gained permission to fish from one bank directly behind the bridge. I had mirrors and commons to 24lb, but I've not finished here yet – a very large common lives here but is proving hard to tempt!

The Priory and Friars Meadows combined make up approximately one mile of river. Friars is part of the Sudbury Common Lands; The Priory stretch is owned by Sudbury and District AA. Therefore there are no silly restrictions. Straight and slow-flowing in normal conditions with depths to eight feet or so, the only frustration is the local rowing club using the stretch to

Robert Gardiner with a 20lb 8oz common at Brundon on the Suffolk Stour.

practise on during daylight. Best here are a 24lb mirror and a 21lb common.

Following on from Friars, it's Pecks Meadows: half a mile of straight and slow-flowing water with a good depth, ending at Bakers Mill and containing a fair head of carp with twenties present. This length is not for me personally owing to the boat traffic, but is worth a try if you can put up with all the Captain Pugwashes! Fishing is on a day ticket through Sudbury and District AA.

Bakers Mill is private but day tickets covering a small area can be purchased from the mill office. Following Bakers Mill is Wright's Meadow, a stretch of one mile with some nice deep bends and absolutely stuffed with carp, mainly smaller fish. However, if you are prepared to wade through the smaller fish there are some bigger ones present. My biggest are a mirror of 25lb and a common of 21lb. It's a long walk from the car park but worth the trek. Sudbury and

District AA control the fishing.

Henny Meadows is another very long stretch ending at Henny Swan, featuring plenty of bends with deep holes. It is under LAA control and holds a good head of carp for anyone willing to trudge a long way from the car park. Opposite Henny Swan is a good-looking weirpool with a very large house called The Floodgates. It's strictly private, but holds some serious carp. I've never tried there; maybe I will soon.

From Henny, it's Lamarsh through to Bures: around four miles of river with lots of interesting stretches. The odd length is controlled by the LAA, the rest being private. I have permission to fish a three-quarter of a mile stretch on the Suffolk bank. It involves a fair drive through farmland to get to the river so I've not spent too much time there, but have still taken fish to 17lb.

Below Bures the river has many interesting stretches, in particular The Rookery. Famous for large chub and roach it is

Brundon Mill on the Suffolk Stour.

Tony Head with a 28lb 2oz carp at Brundon Mill.

known to hold carp, but to what size I don't know. I've never tried it and have never seen anyone else carp fishing there. It is controlled by Sudbury and Earls Colne clubs.

From Bures the river runs through the villages of Fordham and Wormingford on to Nayland. This stretch is mainly open farmland, little of which is controlled by angling clubs, so not much is known about the carp potential.

However, on reaching Nayland we have Wiston Mill. This pool is, in my opinion, the best-looking on the whole of the river, with lovely overhanging willows. It's difficult to access; fishing is from one bank only, and this is about six feet above water level. To the left is a six-step waterfall and the main stream flows directly below where you fish. The pool is directly in front of you, across the other side of the flow. Rods must be positioned high to keep the main line from the current, which is strong enough to move a 4oz lead.

I first started fishing this pool in the win-ter of 1997 and only managed four short sessions, but I was very pleased with the results. I took six fish: doubles of 17lb and 19lb, plus two twenty-one-pounders, a 21lb common and a fully scaled mirror of 24lb. The pool is private but the bank mentioned is controlled by Colchester APS and special permission must be obtained before fishing.

Downstream from Wiston, the river runs under the A134 road from Sudbury to Colchester. This stretch is known as The Cottages and is a long horseshoe-shaped length running round to another bridge heading for Stoke-by-Nayland. There's a fair head of carp. I've only seen fish which I estimate to be 17lb to 19lb in this area, but about four or five years ago a young lad was fishing here for chub with a lump of flake when he hooked a large fish which turned out to be a carp. How he actually landed it on the gear being used I don't know. It was carried into the village to a butcher's shop to be weighed, and turned out to be a common of 33lb. Sadly, the ordeal proved too much for it; on returning the fish to the river it died.

The stretch from Nayland to Boxted is mainly slow-flowing and with a good depth; a very long length of river known to hold carp. I have no real knowledge of this area, having never fished the stretch. The controlling club is Colchester APS.

The same club's stretch from Boxted to Higham is similar – deep and slow-flowing with the odd slightly shallower area. The stretch is reputed to hold carp, but once again I have no first-hand knowledge.

Stratford-St-Mary has lots of private land between Higham and Stratford, but starting at Stratford Bridge, for two meadows up and downstream until just before Dedham Mill, carp can be found. There are some good fish present on this mainly slow stretch, reaching up to the mid-twenties.

Downstream from Stratford the river runs a considerable way before it reaches Flatford Mill. Some very large carp are said to inhabit this pool, but I don't know anyone who has tried for them, mainly because of the public nature of the mill. As some of you may know, it is a very famous landmark with lots of tourists around the place.

Below Flatford the river becomes tidal. It continues on to Manningtree, and shortly after into sea water. I have been told that certain areas below Flatford hold carp to 30lb, but again not much is really known.

CONTACT NUMBERS

Sudbury and District AA	01787 312536
Long Melford AC	01787 377139
Colchester APS	01206 865787
Sudbury Angling Centre	01787 312118

8 The Somerset Levels

Mike Willmott

My river carp fishing stretches back to the mid-1980s, when I was looking for a change, having persevered for over a decade with the lakes and ponds which surrounded me.

The Somerset Levels offers an abundance of man-made drains which have been created over the years to act as an efficient drainage system to prevent thousands of acres of farmland from heavy flooding. Such an area is a rich and natural habitat for many species of wildlife, together with vast stocks of specimen fish.

As the drains are man-made, they cannot be classed as rivers in the true sense of the word; however, I always refer to them as rivers, so please bear with me on this.

The potential of these rivers in terms of maximum growth of carp is still very much unknown; however, there have been carp caught to over 30lb, and with anglers not even having scratched the surface of such venues I think it's fair to say that even bigger fish are distinctly possible.

The natural food chain is certainly sufficient to support such fish, with an absolute abundance of swan mussels, water snails and bloodworm. Further, most stretches of these rivers are littered with aquatic plant life such as wild lilies, Norfolk reeds, Canadian pondweed and underwater cabbages, all of which, to varying degrees, harbour a further abundance of food. In fact, it would be difficult to imagine a more idyllic venue.

The wildlife on these wetlands can be absolutely breathtaking at times, and certainly makes it a pleasure to be there. Kingfishers perching upon the rods is a common occurrence, whilst sharing your swim with the elusive heron is another delight to behold. On more than one occasion I have witnessed wild deer jumping into the water and swimming to the opposite margin just yards away from my hidden presence.

Despite these niceties, very few anglers tend to persevere with any degree of consistency on such venues. However, it must also be said that the fishing can, at times, prove very difficult indeed.

The carp can be extremely nomadic, thus making location very difficult when you consider that they could travel several miles from one day to the next. That said, I have found that most stretches of the rivers do contain some resident fish.

Apart from the carp proving difficult to locate, another stumbling block is the fact that night fishing is not allowed. There are also few access points, and quite often you have to walk for miles across farmland to reach your chosen spot.

Mother Nature can also cause problems. When the heavens open and send down heavy rain, the water levels can build up quite quickly over thousands of acres of flat farmland. Inevitably and purposefully, such water will find its way very quickly into the main drainage systems. This in turn causes a fast rise in the river levels, together with fluctuating water temperatures. Once the water reaches a certain level, the main pumping stations will be alerted and will pump the excess water into the main river system which runs out to sea. Of course, the end result of all this will be fast-flowing water together with all sorts of associated debris. Such conditions make it virtually impossible to fish until the water has been completely pumped away and normal water levels sustained. This can prove extremely frustrating, particularly if you have walked many miles, found the fish and even undertaken a baiting programme. However, in a sadistic kind of way, this is what makes the challenge of river fishing so much more interesting.

Most parts of the river are very silty indeed. This is partly due to the surrounding land being of peat origin, although much of the sediment is the direct result of the floodwater which tends to unsettle the river bed and eventually deposit it. I have found it most advantageous to seek out the firmer spots, which can be few and far between on some stretches.

As with any venue, bait is an important consideration, and due to the fact that these rivers hold a very large head of tench, a little more attention to detail must be given if you are to avoid being plagued with nuisance fish. My initial approach was to use small seeds, such as hemp, tares and groats, as the main carpet of attraction, together with a sparse amount of tiger nuts. I thought such an approach was more natural than boilies, particularly given that up until this time most of the fish had not even seen one.

Hook-baits were two popped-up tiger nuts, these being fished on relatively short hook links of about five inches and enclosed within PVA bags together with carefully dried-out seeds. Using such baits and methods, my results were very encouraging, particularly in terms of action. I caught quite a few carp, mainly between 7lb and 17lb, but also a lot of tench.

This 'chunky' 22lb common was one of many 'virgin' fish during a very successful summer campaign on the river.

The plan was to draw the tench into the swim with the smaller seed and hope that the carp would follow. It certainly worked, but despite the fact that it proved my presentation was correct, I was catching far more tench than I had initially anticipated. I felt this was not only disturbing the swim but also ruining my rig presentation on the firmer spots, which were not easy to find. I also wanted to search out some of the bigger carp I knew were present.

After a while I decided to change tactics and switched to 18mm boilies without the use of any seed whatsoever. I took the risk of using my Creamseed mix; I say risk because despite this bait being one of the most instant carp baits I have ever used, again, the tench also love it. I thought it would be a good test under the circumstances.

My very first outing on the Creamseed mix produced two commons, in pristine

You won't find many dome tents at this venue!

condition, of 18lb and 19lb. I was extremely pleased with such a result as these were very good fish for the river and had probably never been caught before. I only had one tench, but the change of tactics had produced another problem – eels! I caught a couple and also suffered the usual short pulls and missing bait syndrome associated with eel behaviour.

I wanted to try a few more experiments but winter was now fast approaching and the rain was falling with more consistency, resulting in high water levels and running water; not the time for experimenting. The following summer was soon upon us and I decided to wait until there was some settled weather to put my next plan into action. This came in late July, which conveniently fitted in with my son Lee's school holidays.

I always get so much more of a buzz out of my fishing when I take him with me; in fact, not only out of the fishing but out of my surroundings and the wildlife which inhabits it. He takes such a deep interest in what's around him that it's a great form of education for us both and always cements a close bond between us.

After spending several days walking along different stretches of the river in an attempt to find the carp, we eventually found an area we felt confident they were frequenting.

I knew from having used the Creamseed mix the previous year that the carp would instantly accept boilies, so I kept to the same approach, this being without the use of particles to save encouraging nuisance fish.

Mike's son Lee holds a very rare fish, a 22lb 9oz river mirror.

On this occasion though I opted for a prototype fishmeal-based recipe which was eventually launched as my Fish Extract mix. This was used with my Liver Salami and Monster Squid flavours, and I decided to use very big baits – 30mm to be precise!

I was a little dubious about such large baits at first, but when you consider the size of the swan mussels and the excessively large water snails which I had witnessed the carp consume, it all made sense. I air-dried the hook-baits for several days before use, making them rock hard, which I hoped would alleviate the eel problem.

Our plan of attack was to bait up the chosen spots for three days before commencing fishing, then to fish short twelve-hour sessions every third day. I decided to use minimal amounts of bait whilst actually fishing, no more than ten free offerings around each rig, but decided to bait up heavily during the two visits leading up to each session with at least 5lb or 6lb of bait.

The first session produced the required results, with a 21lb 8oz common and a 17lb 8oz mirror. Any fish over 20lb from the drain is an exceptional result, so our hard work and thoughtful planning were certainly well rewarded from the word go.

The next session produced another good fish, this time a 20lb 8oz common, and it was obvious that the large bait approach was accounting for the bigger fish and also combating the tench and eels which in the past were problematic. Our good fortune continued a few days later when we were rewarded with a very rare fish indeed, this being a mirror of 22lb 9oz. Mirrors are rarer still on this particular river; this was only my third ever mirror from this venue.

Another two absolutely pristine, probably uncaught commons, both over 20lb, graced the bank together with a couple of nice upper doubles over the next few sessions, before the carp decided it was time to move on to pastures new.

And so the point was proven: the initial approach of using small seeds and particles certainly produced fish, but none of the bigger carp and plenty of tench. The large bait approach, together with consistent bait application, accounted for the bigger carp on this venue, with five over 20lb in several short visits and none under 17lb, with no nuisance fish whatsoever.

And so the summer drifted away, the carp moved to quieter waters, the rains fell, Lee went back to school, and I settled down for another hard winter carping on a large gravel pit. We haven't been back to the river since, but I know one day we will. Wild untapped waters and virgin carp cannot be ignored for too long.

9 The River Medway

Rob Ness and Gary Peet

Our five-year experience of fishing the River Medway for carp began in 1991. The sections fished were from the flood barrier at Tonbridge down to the Allington Lock at Maidstone, below which the Medway becomes tidal. Between these two points the Medway does not change in character too much, other than getting wider towards Maidstone. Most of the time the Medway is reminiscent of a canal in that the flow is hardly noticeable, so it does not present too many problems in holding bottom and presentation of bait. Having said that, when the rains come, because of the predominantly clay-based catchment area, water quickly runs off the land, turning the river into a raging muddy torrent where you would not expect anything to survive. But of course it does.

We began fishing the Medway independently in 1991, and were both surprised when we met at Maidstone and discovered that there was more than one masochist prepared to potentially sacrifice a season chasing the mythical Medway Carp. In an effort to reduce the steep learning curve of river fishing, we decided to team up and pool our knowledge. Fishing together through the night and the following day, and often a couple of morning or evening sessions each week, the total length of the river that we covered over the four seasons fished was approximately twenty miles, ending in Tonbridge in 1995.

During this period we investigated, researched and fished most sections of the river, though a few pens (a section of river between two locks) were missed, mainly because of inaccessibility or fishing restrictions. Our main approach was to cover different sections each season, concentrating on a couple of pens, though it was often difficult to resist returning to a previously successful swim when new areas were slow to produce.

Above Tonbridge flood barrier the character of the stretch changes to a flowing river and is now more famous for its large barbel. We did not venture into this section to fish for carp because of Gary's fear of bumping into Bob Morris or Peter 'The Eater' Woodhouse. Can you imagine that on a dark autumn evening? Frightening!

During the 1990–91 season Gary fished a lake called Haysden, which is just above the flood barrier at Tonbridge and right next to the River Medway. It was at the end of that season that he decided to fish the Medway for carp. During that close season Gary realized he had not looked forward to the start of a season with so much anticipation for a long time. The challenge seemed greater than the previous few seasons, and the thought of landing uncaught carp, his main drive in carp fishing, gave a new incentive to his preparations. Gary made regular visits to the Maidstone section and bought a boat with which to survey the river. Using a Minn Kota outboard and fish finder that had previously been used for reservoir pike fishing, the messing about on the river sometimes seemed more fun than the fishing itself. In the following years, though it proved itself to be an indispensable piece of equipment, the boat was at times a distraction from efficient fishing.

How many fish were disturbed from swims as the boat churned up and down the river?

With the use of a wooden pole for feeling the bottom, Gary searched the areas that were considered good spots. He hoped that his earlier years spent fishing for chub on the River Darent had set him in good stead to interpret the information he was collecting. Gary did not know if prebaiting would have the desired effect, so concentrating on good location was to be the key for the first session.

A fish of about 5lb had been seen in the Allington Marina the week before and this tilted the balance – a session opposite the marina entrance marked the start of the season. One of Gary's mates, Clive, accompanied him for this first session. He also helped make bait and carried out the baiting-up a few days before the trip. It was a long way to carry all the kit, so the boat was used to transport it. This made the journey effortless. Gary's diary shows that it was the evening of 17 June, and they were soon set up, settled and drinking their first cuppa. The prospect of getting a take appeared daunting. It seemed highly unlikely that carp would find the bait, bearing in mind the length of the river, and in fact there might not be any carp within a mile of the baits. The results of this first session were a surprise to both Gary and Clive. At midnight on the first night, Gary hooked and landed a common of 5lb – a pleasing start. However, it was during the daylight hours of the following morning, around 8am, that Gary hooked and landed a superb fish of 19lb 12oz, a fully scaled mirror. The scene was set for the coming season.

Though Clive fished a number of sessions, he never caught a river carp. His dedication to making bait, carrying kit and netting fish was often rewarded by being allowed to return Gary's fish. Cheers Clive!

Rob moved to Kent from Dorset during the winter of 1990–91. Looking for a fresh carp-fishing challenge, the local waters appeared heavily fished, and with transport initially limited to the Maidstone locality there were few options available. During the spring of 1991, whilst looking out of his office window (two metres from the tow-path of the Medway), he spotted a number of fish spawning in a large weedbed on the far bank. The new season's venue had been decided.

The weedbed swim bordered a large overhanging alder tree; it was to this feature that the carp seemed attracted. Upon investigation, the roots of the tree and the weedbed itself were found to be a haven for various snails and crustaceans, and the silt plateau on which the weedbed was growing contained large numbers of small-sized swan mussels. In order to be able to effectively fish the swim, an area of two metres by one metre of weed was cleared. The far edges of the cleared area were then marked with sticks pushed into the silt, and the area baited two to three times a week with maples and scopex-flavoured boilies during the month running up to the start of the season.

Many fish were observed moving within the weedbed, mostly in the low double category. The swim appeared to be a holding area, with fish being present throughout the day, often staying for long periods of time on the surface between gaps in the weed. Even large passing boats, which created bow waves that rocked the river, failed to disturb the fish from their basking activities.

Rob's first session of the season began at 6am in daylight; fishing alone in the dark was not an activity that Rob enjoyed! Two rods were used and pop-up scopex boilies were positioned in the cleared area within the weedbed. The first take was quick in coming, the first fish to be landed being a small common of around 7lb. By the amount of movement within the weedbed, there were obviously several fish within the swim. Line bites were a constant problem, mainly due to the lines having laid across the surface of the weed prior to entering the

Gary Peet with a 20lb+ linear mirror fron the River Medway.

water at a steep angle through the gap in the weed.

The next fish hooked was lost soon after connection, the fish ploughing deep into the weed. Even after this commotion fish were still observed moving undisturbed through the swim. Right under the rod tops, in no more than eighteen inches of water, a large fish was spotted moving slowly through the channels within the weed. A pop-up, set at around five or six inches off the bottom, was positioned in the channel, with the bait aimed directly in the path of the fish for interception – easier to eat the bait than move round it? As planned, the fish swam up to the bait, the take was not seen, and the water erupted as the fish tore into the tangle of weed. Rob grabbed the net and jumped into the water. The fish made little progress due to the density of the weed and

the pressure put on it. Soon the fish was wallowing on the surface and was netted. On returning to the bank the size of the fish could be fully appreciated – an old-looking chestnut brown mirror, in perfect condition, at 23lb 6oz.

It was a tremendous start to the river campaign, but perhaps gave a false impression of how easy future fishing might be …

BAIT

We caught on most baits, including bird foods, protein baits, tigers and maples. It was bait application that was of most importance. We found that prebaiting worked exceptionally well because the carp seemed to be nomadic and would visit the obvious features along the length of river.

When we prebaited we were effectively holding wandering carp by creating or improving a feeding location, so that when we fished the swim we were fishing for a larger head of carp than would normally be there. There were so few carp anglers on the river, it was relatively easy to openly bait up and fish without competition for swims. We noticed that when we did two nights on the trot we invariably had better results on the second night.

The routine was for Rob to bait up on Wednesdays and Sundays with two kilos of boilies, five kilos of hemp, five kilos of mixed tigers, maples and maize, and to fish Monday nights and Tuesdays until midnight. The mix used for baiting up was approximately 25 per cent tigers, 25 per cent maples and 50 per cent maize. We preferred the maize and maples fermented, but the hemp and tigers were used fresh.

The method of preparation of these particles was as follows: the maples were soaked for approximately twenty-four hours, then allowed to sit for a further day or two until the seeds began to germinate. At this point they were boiled for twenty to thirty minutes until the peas were soft, then semi-drained and allowed to cool. To further enhance the attraction of the bait (and if the wife and neighbours didn't mind), we allowed the baits to ferment in any of the remaining liquid for a couple of days, then bagged them and froze them. The hemp was soaked for approximately twenty-four hours, the water changed three or four

Rob Ness with a blotchy 20lb mirror.

times to clean the dirt and dust away. Then we added a pinch of salt, brought them to the boil and simmered them for five minutes. We let them cool, then drained and packed them in bags before freezing. With maize, no benefit was found by soaking for twenty-four hours. It seemed not to take on any noticeable amount of water. So we just brought it to the boil, again added salt and left it to simmer for between thirty and sixty minutes, the length of time dependent on how hard or soft and fluffy the maize was required to be.

You will find bags of maize for sale marked 'Whole Maize' that vary with regard to the actual percentage of whole seeds they contain. The split seeds become soft and fluffy very quickly during boiling and you end up with a mixture of hard and soft maize. The soft, fluffy maize helps to attract the silver fish and acts in conjunction with the hemp to create a feeding frenzy. The harder seeds are left for the larger fish such as chub, bream and carp. However, a mixture of soft and hard maize is a problem if catapulted because the hard maize goes further than the soft maize. For distance, a boat or carrier such as balls of white crumb should be used. Once boiled, the maize should be left to ferment in a sealed bucket for approximately one week until it produces a slightly cheesy smell. We believe that this is when maize is at its best. It would then be drained, bagged and frozen.

Gary liked to prepare tigers over a longer period, soaking for four days and changing the water every day. This process helps enlarge the tigers to their fullest extent due to the osmotic difference between the clean water and the tiger nut. We would then boil them for between fifteen and thirty minutes, leave to cool, drain and then bag and freeze. Don't use any salt in the preparation of nuts as the salt appears not to penetrate them and inhibits the uptake of water. Basically, they taste the same with or without salt. With seed baits it's different. If you pre-

pare two batches of seeds with and without salt you will understand our reasons for using salt. However, take care not to use too much as it could act as a deterrent.

The boilies we used were varied. We prepared our own base mixes, from fishmeal base to bird food to protein. Flavours included Scopex (Hutchinson), Esterblend 12 (Solar), Ming Oil (Tackle Box), Juicy Peach (DT Baits), and, most successfully, a fishmeal/milk protein base in conjunction with Condensed Milk Flavour (obtained from Lee Jackson), Squid and Octopus Koi Rearer (Solar) and a Liquid Atlantic Krill Extract (an additive that was available to Rob). We changed baits each season because we got bored making the same bait; however, there is no doubt that our results suffered from this constant changing. There were two reasons for this: firstly, the river is not the place to field test new flavours or ideas, and secondly, unless supervised closely the agreed recipe would be modified by Gary, never to its benefit! Once we actually collected swan mussels by the bucketload and used them in the preparation of boilies, but found it was a lot of hard work for what seemed to be a lower catch rate.

RECIPES

Here are just a couple of the most successful mixes used on the river.

Scopex Special
(Per kilogram dry mix/11 size 1 eggs. Boil for ninety seconds.)

400g Ground salmon flavoured cat biscuit
200g 30 mesh casein
150g Full-fat soya flour
150g Semolina
100g Ground hemp
40ml Sesame oil
12ml Scopex
10ml Juicy Peach

Fish Mix

(Per kilogram dry mix/13 size 1 eggs. Boil for ninety seconds.)

600g Hi Nu Val (Nutrabaits) or Protein Mix (Tackle Box)
200g Mixed fishmeal (one third White Fishmeal, one third Capelin Meal, one third Sardine & Anchovy Meal)
100g Full-fat soya flour
100g Semolina
5ml Squid and Octopus Koi Rearer
10ml Condensed Milk Flavour
35ml Liquid Atlantic Krill Extract
20ml Olive oil

Hook-baits used included tiger nuts, maize, various boilie-based pop-ups and bottom baits, and snowman rigs. In the main, 16mm baits were used.

The one aspect of river carp fishing that is different to stillwater fishing and should be remembered and used to the angler's advantage, is the potential to use the flow of the river to distribute and advertise the food label of the bait. This does not mean over-dosing the baits with flavours, though it was found acceptable to use a higher level of flavour than may be considered normal for stillwaters. High local concentrations of leached flavours do not build up, due to the river flow. Using higher levels of natural attractors and flavours, such as the Liquid Krill Extract within boilies and as a soak for particles, appeared to be particularly effective. On numerous occasions single baits cast in whilst setting up were taken almost immediately.

During a session we also found it important to bait the swim at regular intervals. The effect of the flow and the wash created by passing boats can disturb and move baits, particularly those of low density. A top up after boats have passed is a good approach, though this has to be carried out sensibly to prevent overbaiting. When fishing in or between weedbeds there is less of a need to follow the baiting method described, as the weed acts as a buffer to the effects of water movement.

LOCATION

The most productive areas are reasonably obvious to identify. These include bridges, marinas, weedbeds, snags, large eddies (which we called lay byes) and overhanging trees. The less obvious locations are not visible. These include deep holes. Although we've never caught from a deep hole, carp seem to congregate around or near them, perhaps as a safe haven when the river floods? If I was given the choice of fishing a snag near a deep hole, or a snag away from a deep hole, I would choose the former. A section of river with a definite sheer drop to its bank and a consistent depth for a continued distance, perhaps twenty or thirty yards, also seemed to hold a good head of carp. We also found very rocky areas productive. In fact, on one swim we fished, the number of rocks prevented retrieval of our leads. We had to wait for a take or use the boat to get above the lead so we could retrieve the end tackle. Our theory, based on observation, is that the rocks hold snails and other food items that shelter between the rocks and graze on the algae that grow on them. Carp appear to visit these areas regularly, perhaps to see if any snails are out of their trenches?

WHERE TO PLACE YOUR BAIT

The centre of the river is not the place to catch carp. We have only caught fish from the centre when there has been a feature to fish to, such as a weedbed or a rock formation. In 90 per cent of cases the most productive areas to fish were those with either natural or man-made features on either margin, such as weedbeds.

The dense weedbeds created by Potamogeton, a dark green crispy leaf which tends to grow in water between six and thirty inches deep, were found to be particularly productive. There are a number of these beds in the Maidstone to East Farleigh sections, and without exception fish were either caught or observed in these areas. The fish obviously felt secure in this enclosed environment, and could be observed in close quarters moving through or basking within the narrow channels that they had furrowed within the weed. This weed is an oxygenating type, and on sunny days bubbles of released oxygen could be observed as they reached the surface, either naturally or due to disturbance by fish or tackle. It may be that it is the higher localized oxygen content of the surrounding water that is attractive to the fish. This would explain their presence during daylight, when oxygen is released, and their absence from these weedbeds at night, when the weed absorbs oxygen.

Presenting bait was done by dropping bait with some free offerings into one of the clear channels. Takes were usually pre-empted by the movement of the weed as the fish moved in. However, extraction of the fish once hooked was not always an easy job. When fishing such swims we would advocate the use of 15lb main line, with rods and terminal tackle matched to the situation and able to cope with the hook and hold tactics required.

Weedbeds of the streamer type are common throughout the length of the river. Again, these areas were found to be productive, especially where large beds had grown and formed clear bays within the main mass of the bed. The Nettlestead section of the river and upstream to Yalding held a number of such swims, which proved to be particularly productive. One word of

warning: because this type of weedbed is so common, picking the right one can be a daunting prospect. Look for areas that have other notable features, such as shallow plateaux, a deep hole, or trees or bushes which overhang or grow into the water. Spotting fish in the weedbed is obviously the best prompt for choice of swim.

In the East Farleigh to Teston section there were different types of weedbed. They were large beds formed from a number of different types of weed and incorporating various types of lilies. Such beds can be found on the far bank upstream from East Farleigh opposite the mobile home park, and another further upstream on the towpath side, known locally as the bomb hole. Both these swims provided plenty of takes; however, generally in this section the fish were of a smaller size than other areas fished.

Along the length of the Medway there are several marinas. The fish seem to have an affinity with marinas. We found it almost impossible to get permission to fish within a marina. However, success was gained by fishing opposite the marinas, especially those which incorporated boat-holding bays off the main river. The fish seemed to associate with these bays, using them as sanctuaries away from the main river and the steady procession of boats which cruise up and down during the day. Fish were often observed basking in these bays on sunny days. By carefully positioning baits into the mouth of such entrances, although these are not natural feeding areas for the fish, opportunist feeding fish moving in and out of the marina could often be caught. Care must be taken when casting in such areas as the potential risk of damage caused by a stray cast makes boat owners nervous, and can lead to difficult situations.

If a boat is being used, baits can be positioned within the marinas more easily. This again can lead to confrontation with boat/marina owners if discretion is not used.

The carrying out of such SAS tactics often leads to the capture of fish on days that would otherwise have been unproductive.

Those marinas fished with success included the two upstream from Allington locks (takes came from the entrances or just inside the bays); along the boat-lined section at Wateringbury marina; Yalding Marina, especially during flood conditions; and the area around the small marina in the Tonbridge town section.

Snags provide another important feature for the location of river carp. The Medway is generally well maintained; however, within most sections notable snags can be found that often hold relatively large numbers of fish. Trees that have fallen into the river, usually from bank erosion caused by the heavy boat traffic, and are either dead or alive, can provide good sport, particularly when baiting up has taken place.

There are two or three swims in the Maidstone Cattle Market area containing partially submerged trees and bushes. There are also a similar number of features in the Nettlestead and Tonbridge sections, from which a high proportion of the fish caught over the four years were taken. When walking the river these snag swims are fairly obvious, and more often than not scream 'fish me!'

Gary's method of fishing snags, learnt during his time fishing for chub, was to position baits on the downstream side of the snag, as experience showed this to be the more productive side. The thinking behind this theory is that a snag creates a slowing of the flow and an opportunity for suspended silt and foodstuffs to settle, forming a silt pocket and an area in which fish are likely to feed. Gary's results from fishing this method compared to Rob's 'either side will do' method appear to justify his tactic.

Old wooden boat moorings, platforms and sunken boats also offer a holding area for fish; more so if the structures are not in regular use. The Allington section has many far bank swims with old moorings and collapsing platforms from which fish were caught. East Farleigh also has numerous boat moorings.

Bridges were initially considered to be the likely river hotspots. We had read and been told that river carp usually congregate around such structures. However, in our experience, other than a notable carp that was often seen around Tovil footbridge and a small shoal of mid-doubles which held around the railway bridge in Tonbridge (one of which was caught), no fish were seen at other bridges. Despite many sessions spent fishing bridge swims, no fish, other than the one exception, were caught. However, this is only our experience, and anyone fishing the Medway should not discount such features.

Without a doubt, the bottom of the marginal shelf is a very productive area. If you are using a boat, the marginal shelf can be found using a long wooden stick. You can feel the shelf as it slopes down, and at the bottom is an area that collects small waterlogged sticks, stones, snail shells and other such debris. This can actually be located through the vibrations of the stick, and can also be felt through careful leading with your rod. The area may only be six inches wide, but this is where a lot of the natural food collects and is therefore a very effective place to put your hook-bait.

We found that carp and other fish generally patrol this band of richness, grubbing and mooching about looking for a meal. This band of rubble enlarges at different parts of the river, such as lay byes, the inside edges of bends and the downstream side of a snag.

Where features previously described can be located in conjunction with a marginal shelf, the ideal spot for bait positioning may have been located, though as with any form of fishing it is not an exact science and the details given in this text are only a guide. The finding of a prolific hotspot does require an amount of trial and error, as well as the associated tears and pain.

FEEDING TIMES

Experience over the four years on the Medway showed that during the summer and autumn the carp mostly fed between dusk and dawn. During these periods baits fished on the bottom seemed to be the most effective, but during the day it became more difficult to get a take in the majority of features previously described. We found that a six-inch pop-up, carefully positioned in gaps or channels within weedbeds, with a few free offerings, was one way of achieving the odd take during daylight. It was often possible to intercept fish as they cruised from weedbed to weedbed on the near bank, or more predominantly on the far bank. In one or two feet of water the fish seemed happy to accept and eat baits presented in such a manner, though heavy baiting in such circumstances definitely did not work; all they would seem to accept was a small snack.

In winter, the balance of takes again seemed to favour the hours of darkness, with most fish being taken between dusk and midnight.

We would be very surprised to see a monster come from the Medway (a monster being a fish in excess of 35lb). The biggest fish we caught were two of 25lb – but don't be mistaken, we hold these fish in very high esteem. We chose to fish for these uncaught

The River Medway, showing the water level down. Rob and Gary photographed long lengths of the river like this to show bank-side features.

doubles and twenties rather than fish on circuit waters that hold twenties, thirties or even forties.

The general size of fish you can expect to catch is from low to mid-doubles. These are quite common, but upper doubles are few and far between. We would catch maybe six or seven upper doubles a year, fishing one day and night a week and odd morning and evening sessions. Twenties? Well! The river only saw fit for us to catch a total of thirteen – three or four a year. However, someone with more time would surely achieve better results than we did, especially if the more productive areas were concentrated on, rather than our approach of catch a few and move on.

The largest carp caught that we know of, other than the inevitable rumours, was a 27lb mirror taken by Ken Crow on sweetcorn during flood conditions at a marina near Yalding.

We only saw one fish bigger than those we caught – a fish certainly over 30lb – but despite considerable effort we never managed to catch that fish, although it was seen in its usual holding spot as recently as 1997. Perhaps we will try for it again next year. Overall, we would imagine that there are one or two thirties currently swimming in the Medway. Wherever they are would have to be a safe haven during flood conditions, and would also need to provide an area of sufficient depth to survive the occasional draining of sections by the river authority to facilitate lock repairs. Any ideas?

With two people fishing once a week we would expect to catch, on average, one or two carp per session. However, blanks are a very real prospect, but then so are multiple catches. The best session we experienced was nine takes with seven fish landed. On two occasions we both caught twenties dur-

Rob with a cracking brace of river carp.

ing the same session, culminating in the capture of commons of 25lb 6oz and 24lb 12oz in the Tonbridge section in the early season of 1994.

Summary of Fish Caught

Allington to East Farleigh: 8 twenties, 19 doubles, 12 singles.

East Farleigh to Teston: 0 twenties, 7 doubles, 12 singles.

Teston to Yalding: 2 twenties, 16 doubles, 11 singles.

Yalding to Tonbridge town lock: 0 twenties, 6 doubles, 13 singles.

Tonbridge town lock to flood barrier: 3 twenties, 14 doubles, 9 singles.

RIGS

We prefer the type of lead that hangs off the side of the line, the main reason being that this set-up allows you to feel the bottom more effectively. For us to know what type of bottom we were fishing on was very important. The best system found for this purpose was the Nash Safety Bead, which allows the lead to be released if the fish swims through snags. The bead is adjusted by cutting the lip from where the lead sits and fitting a loose tail rubber to the rear of the clip to connect to the tubing. This helps the lead to release with less effort.

The hair rig used was quite basic by today's standards – a simple knotless knot with 12lb Big Game and a size six or four Drennan Super Specialist or later Ashima C310, with a hook link length of approximately six to ten inches depending upon the situation.

There is a lot of boat traffic on the Med-

way in the summer, and at least one boat will usually pass you even on the worst winter's day. This means that you will need to use backleads when fishing the far margin. This also helps avoid most floating snags as they do not normally hug the margins. For a backlead we used a weight of at least 1oz, as lighter leads had a greater tendency to move in the slight and variable current of the river. Also, a heavier backlead transfers any bite indication back to the bobbin more efficiently. Light backleads seem to lift up until you get a straight line, before any bite indication is registered.

The backlead clip still used by both of us is a modified plastic-coated paperclip. We have not seen any manufactured clips that improve on this design. If the lead becomes snagged the paperclip opens up and releases the main line, with the fish hopefully still attached. The bobbins used for this were the hanger types of about half to three-quarters of an ounce. These seemed to be about adequate to counteract the flow of the river, but still indicated movement before the 1oz backlead moved. We used 3oz leads on the rig because the action of putting on the backlead could move the position of the carefully placed rig if a lighter lead was used.

Most boat traffic respects anglers, but sometimes their desire not to disturb you can lead you to despair. It is quite common to have boats move to the far side of the river to avoid you. We once encountered a boat that moved so tight to the far bank in an effort to minimize our disturbance that he ploughed through the weedbed being fished and his propeller picked up all three of the baits. How's that for multiple takes!

The occasional canoeist can also cause problems. There can be no doubt that a canoeist with attitude seems to purposely go through anglers' lines, and unfortunately there seemed to be a large number with this disposition. The advantage to today's angler fishing the Medway is that many of the canoeists in the areas we fished are now suitably educated in the virtues of 15lb Big Game!

Generally, don't worry about the boats disturbing your fishing. The fish are quite used to their presence. In fact, more than once we had a take from under a boat that always seemed to have a party going on inside! And during another period we failed to get a morning take until the first boat had passed.

SUMMARY

The seasons we spent on the Medway were both exciting and fulfilling with respect to the fishing. Every take was an opportunity to catch a previously uncaught fish, monster or not, and although we never did get beyond the 25lb mark, every fish was a triumph in itself. Neither of us had begun fishing the Medway with ambitions beyond just catching a river carp or two, and proving all the doubters and cynics wrong. With our initial aims achieved, we set about looking for the bigger fish. We managed to catch a few, and in the process learned and developed the techniques to catch these sometimes elusive fish, and, more importantly, enjoyed the fishing.

At the end of the 1995 season, having covered the majority of the accessible and interesting sections of the river, we decided to conclude fishing the Medway and look for new venues to fish. Rob still spends the start of each season fishing the odd session after the one specific fish, to date unsuccessfully, whilst Gary focused his efforts, with some notable results, on catching the carp in the Kentish Rother.

10 The Royal Military Canal: The Beginning

Bill Phillips

A love affair resulting in a marriage that lasted a decade best describes my passion for the Royal Military Canal (RMC) during the 1970s. Even now, nearly thirty years later, as I reflect on those years I feel a tingling in my spine and a tear in my eyes. There are mixed emotions of sadness for the loss of an irretrievable magic, and joy for having experienced such a personal, passionate relationship with such a wonderful water. I am sitting at my desk, surrounded by diaries, books, notes and photographs associated with those times. Strangely, as if it were yesterday, I can smell the water, the grass, trees, even the 'fishy' scent that only the habitual angler can understand. And the sound of the relentless croaking of the frogs at dawn, the chattering of birds as they seek their evening roost in the elms, along with the roar of lions as they are fed at the nearby Port Lympne wildlife park. My mind's eye is dominated at this moment by the slightest flicking of the lily pads, causing rings of ripples around individual pads, the occasional light plop as a pad is submerged, this clearly betraying the presence of those elusive blue torpedoes. Oh, what wonderful memories!

Alas, so much has now changed. The romance and mystery have long gone, along with the beautiful elms (decimated by Dutch Elm disease in the seventies). Even the frogs are considerably depleted. A change in the controlling club has allowed a large part of the canal's length to fall into disrepair. However, the stories I have to tell in the following pages are from those magic years of the seventies, a time when carp anglers were truly habitually striving against all the odds. They rose to the challenges, solved the mysteries and enjoyed their failures far, far more than many of today's carp catchers enjoy their successes.

The Royal Military Canal is deep in the south-east of England, running from Iden Lock in the west, eastward to Shorncliffe Sluice. It was planned as a defence against the invasion of Napoleon in 1804. In reality, it was built to provide a navigable waterway and line of defence nineteen miles long. It was finished in August 1806, far too late to have been effective against the invasion, had it been mounted by Napoleon in 1804 or 1805. In 1867 the Secretary of State for War sold the RMC as it was no longer considered necessary. The buyers were a body responsible for the drainage of the Romney Marshes. Around this time, due to there being a second controlling body (Hythe Corporation), the canal was split into two. In 1873 the division of the canal into two sections was consolidated by the building of the Lympne Dam, followed by the sluice in 1883, which enabled water from the marshes to drain into the canal and be diverted to the sea. The last barge travelled the RMC in 1909 and, ironically, in 1940 the War Office requisitioned the canal and built many pill boxes along its length as a defence against Hitler.

By the 1950s, the canal's main functions were drainage and pleasure. Many trees had been planted, dominated by 12,500 elms. Fish had been stocked, including a consignment of carp from the Surrey Trout Farm in 1956, some of which I am sure are the big mirrors that still exist. However, there were carp in the RMC long before this, confirmed by the following quote from the Tiffin Guide to Hythe of 1816:

> The Royal Military Canal was stocked with fish in 1806 and, having been carefully guarded and never fished, abounds with large carp, tench, perch, pike, eels and other freshwater fish. Licences for angling are expected shortly to be granted, as fishing these waters is advertised to be let by lease.

During the late nineteenth and early twentieth century, the RMC was recognized for its 'wild carp' fishing, particularly in the Hythe area. The then well-known Walker's Tackle Shop in Hythe had a stuffed 8lb fish caught in 1911 on display. I believe this fish now resides in the Hythe Royal British Legion Club. Knowledge of stocking records is limited, partly due to the loss of the Southern Water Authority (SWA) records when the National Rivers Authority took over in the late 1980s. Among the records I have managed to trace, stocking of carp has varied tremendously. Farm pond wildies and Surrey Trout Farm mirrors in the 1940s and 1950s; SWA Italian mirrors in the 1960s; Wadhurst wildies in the 1970s; common carp from Eastwell Lake in 1974; 500 mirrors from SWA in 1984, and even grass carp in 1984/85. In spite of a few losses of fish over the years, due to oxygen levels and pollution on several occasions, the worst recorded as decimating fish stock in the Ashford Angling Club section in 1958, I believe the RMC still holds many good carp to this day. I also reckon that there are a few secrets the canal has yet to reveal. But I do not think that many of the modern-day carp anglers have the ability or the inclination to discover those secrets, if indeed they exist, which in my book is the major attraction – the unknown!

Let me take you back to a time when all fishing was magical – childhood. I must have been about twelve years old and lived in the village of Sellindge, about seven miles from the RMC. Rods tied to the cross-bar of my bike with binder twine, a wicker basket on my back, most weekends and holidays would see me pedalling frantically towards the canal. The journey took me from the main A20, along Otterpool Lane and past Lympne Airport. One of the highlights was the descent of Lympne Hill, a steep, long and, in hindsight, very dangerous activity. Often, I would be with my fishing mate, Steve. We would set ourselves at the top, as if on a starting grid, and then race like lunatics to the bottom, the prize being first choice of swim. Unfortunately, it often resulted in parting company with bikes, injuries or tackle damage. Stupid, but we still did it and miraculously never really got hurt. Probably the worst pain was at the end of a long day, weighted down with tackle – it took a good half an hour to push the bike back up that wretched hill.

The section of the RMC that ran along the bottom of the hill was known as West Hythe, and was controlled by Cinque Ports Angling Club. The main reason for fishing there was because it was the closest to my home. The water was shallow, weedy and rather murky. In those oh so happy days, nothing seemed to matter. There was always the feeling of anticipation that we would catch a monster. We never did, but the enthusiasm was relentless. My tackle consisted of bamboo rods and an Intrepid reel. Favourite floats were of the Grayling type; I am sure that was due to the way the rings of ripples were produced as they bobbed. Occasionally, a really good bite would be heard as the float plopped under. What a lovely sound that was!

We often caught lots of small roach, bream, perch, occasionally a tench, and then pike in the winter. Never, in those days, did we catch carp. We knew of them, but had read, heard and believed that they

74

were almost uncatchable. We even had to talk about them in a slow whisper. It is so strange now to reflect on the mystery that the word 'carp' encompassed. Very occasionally, what were believed to be monster carp were seen, deep and blue, usually drifting under the old brick road bridge, which was so often a vantage point to be fished from.

It must have been about 1961/62 when I was first infected by the carp virus. I didn't know it at the time, but it is embedded in my memory. The day was hot and still. I was fishing alone at West Hythe, bored at the lack of action in the heat of the midday sun. I became aware of a presence on the opposite bank, an almost ghost-like figure crouched between two elder bushes. He was obviously fishing, but what a daft place to try to fish I remember thinking. Eventually, well pretty quickly, curiosity encouraged me to go round and have a look. As I approached from the bank above, I could smell his pipe. It was gently puffing clouds of grey smoke that hovered around him like a mist. 'What are you doing, mister?' I asked. 'Carp, lad. Carp,' was the slow, hushed, yet determined answer. He somehow produced an air that made me sit low and quiet, but also a magnetic field that would not release me. I sat and studied. His tackle was simple, but looked strong. Where was his float? All I could see were some large chunks of bread in the marginal lilies to his right. Occasionally he would slowly lift his hand, point and whisper: 'There.' This confused me, but I did not ask, just nodded knowingly.

Gradually, over the weeks of that summer, I got to know a little about this strange fellow. His name was Ron and he was fishing floating crust for carp. Only once did I see him catch, and that was a wild carp of some 6lb. This virtual stranger, and the awesome fish I saw him land, had a deep and lasting impression. I was infected for life and, in fact, became a carrier of the

incurable carp fever. I wonder if he knew or, indeed, if he is still alive. The virus lay semi-dormant for several years while I served a long, enjoyable apprenticeship acquiring the skills of the art of angling. Wherever and for whatever I fished, even when successful, Ron and his carp would still haunt me.

The year 1969 was a watershed. I was fishing a beautiful stretch of the RMC at Aldergate, mainly for tench. I had read a lot about carp and, indeed, caught a few in local ponds. Ashford Angling Club had control of the fishing between Iden lock and West Hythe Dam, some fourteen to fifteen miles. This was my favoured stretch of water, full of character and very pretty. The remaining stretch from the dam to Shorncliffe, some five miles or so, was controlled by Cinque Ports Angling Club. This length was unattractive, weedy, shallow, dirty and far too urban for me to consider. However, even as early as the mid-sixties there were reports of carp into the low twenties from the Hythe area. More about the Hythe carp fishing can be read in the chapter on the Royal Military Canal by Richard and Steve Howkins.

Aldergate is between Gigger's Green Bridge and the West Hythe Dam, a distance of three to four miles without the interruption of a road bridge. This made it the most secluded and undisturbed length of the canal. It was in the mid-reaches of Aldergate, the farthest walk from the bridges, that I first discovered the consistent presence of what by now had become my quarry. What a magnificent stretch of water! To this day, the prettiest I have ever fished. With open fields to the south, the canal nestled into the base of a steep hillside to the north. Bedded into this hillside was Port Lympne wildlife park, the noises from which added a more intense eeriness when fishing alone as darkness fell. The ruins of Stutfall Castle and the serenity of Lympne Castle were among the treasures that the north bank possessed. Fishing from the north bank was not allowed. It was mostly thick with trees, many of which overhung the water. Undergrowth was dominated by briars and hawthorn that smelled sweet in the early summer. High and heavy bulrushes to much of the margins completed the backdrop.

During the summer season, the water was often fairly clear, with depths of three to four feet in the margins, shelving rapidly to eight to nine feet in the centre. The average width of fifty to sixty feet was largely occupied by fifteen-foot-wide margins of beautiful lesser yellow waterlilies to both banks. They were so thick that moorhens would walk on them. There were masses of yellow flowers, doing impressions of floating king cups, fringed on the banks by yellow flag irises. The lilies were a large part of the canal's character as a fishery. Most anglers hated them, finding it near impossible to fish without cutting out a swim. For me, they did so much to assist, both when fishing and when observing. The clarity of the water was partly due to lilies acting as a sunshade. Carp loved to bask in them, and they were a very reliable means of portraying the presence of carp gliding among their stems and feeding on the snails adhered to the underside of the leaves.

In spite of seeing several of what, at the time, I considered to be massive carp, and indeed witnessing a couple of very short accidental encounters where friends were snapped up on float gear, it was not until the 1970 season that I started fishing for them in earnest. At the time, I often wondered if I was the only carp angler in the world, and if it really was possible to catch those blue torpedoes I so often saw. Over the next three years I spent nearly 700 hours failing to actually land a single canal carp. Some of my efforts were obscure to say the least – wearing rubber gloves to bait up, camouflage tackle, a deckchair for long sessions (because wood was less noisy than the metal type of chair), and candles in jam jars to light up Fairy Liquid bottle top indicators, with bananas, cherries, carrot cubes and blackberries for bait. I even went through a period of preconditioning tinned potatoes by leaving them in the canal for several days so that they contained water bugs before I would use them on the hook. This was after two of my very few hooked fish came to potato that had been in the water for over twenty-four hours. Floating crust, particularly in the marginal lilybeds, was one of my more conventional and nearly successful methods.

I guess I hooked and lost about half a dozen carp between 1970 and 1973. Most were lost due to my being unable to cope with their terrific speed and awesome power, coupled with the density of the lilybeds. Truth be known, it was lack of experience and inadequate tackle.

By 1973 I had built up a considerable knowledge of both water and carp. Even though I had not banked one, I knew that most of them were commons up to mid-teens and that a few big mirrors existed, two of which I knew well. One had a white spot on its shoulder, so I called it White Spot (pathetic, isn't it?). Incidentally, I was never to catch that fish, but I caught the other big mirror twice, a fish that became my personal best and remains my best ever capture bar none …

The close season had been spent preparing a couple of swims in the most remote area of the Aldergate length. The banks sloped steeply to the water's edge, making it difficult to fish close to the water. To overcome this, I dug the bank out to allow my deckchair and tackle to fit in a nice flat pitch, level with the water. One of the two dugouts was made larger to accommodate an occasional companion, Doug White, who was to join me for the opening few days. Signs were put up with the words: 'Prebaited swim. Please do not fish. Bill Phillips'. No one ever did. Wouldn't it be nice if such honour existed nowadays?

Sheep hurdles were laid over the top of the dugouts, then sacking and finally turf so as to obscure the fact that beneath was a cave-like den. Rushes were planted in front of the swim to obscure the presence of yours truly. Channels were cut in the marginal lilies. These were regularly cut throughout the following season, and indeed for a number of years.

Over the next few years, the big swim was encroached upon by a family of badgers and became a sett which exists to this day. More of this later, but those badgers, along with many other wild creatures, became a fascinating part of my life as an habitual carp angler on the Royal Military Canal.

The start of the 1973 season was historic in my angling career. It is best described using an excerpt from an article that I wrote for a magazine called *Osmos*:

On Sunday 17 June 1973, I finished work at 23:00 and set off to fish a swim on the Royal Military Canal, a heavily fished day ticket water run by the Ashford Angling Club. I had been prebaiting a swim with bread and tinned potatoes for about three weeks. My first outing to the swim on opening night (00:30, 16 June) had been unproductive and very cold. By the time I reached the swim, the moon was bright and the weather very fine. I had decided to fish for carp. Conditions were good for this type of fishing. There is a small head of carp in the canal, but they are very, very rarely caught. In fact, Ashford Angling Club have not weighed one in officially for over ten years. I tackled up my Mk IV carp rod and Mitchell carp reel. A baiting needle was used to thread a potato up the 8lb BS line before securing a size four hook. With the line cast, my bite alarm set and candle burning, I settled down for the night.

The first few hours went by and I began nodding off. At 00:30, the sound of my Heron alarm woke me with a start. I grabbed for the rod but it was gone. A mad panic, and I retrieved it from the water only to find that the line had snapped. Not too long after came another run, this one I hit. A mirror carp of considerable size, at least 15lb, could be seen in the torch light thrashing about in the weeds. Played out, it was ready for the net which was held by my mate Doug. It spat the hook. God, how my hands were shaking, with a heartbeat to match!

A long wait and another fast take, followed by a short, but lively, fight, resulted in the capture of my first ever RMC carp. A wildie weighing in at 4lb 12oz. I don't expect anyone reading this to understand the enormity of that small carp. My duck has been broken. This was the only time in my life I would ever catch my first Royal Military Canal carp. At 08:00 – bang! All hell let loose. I was into a biggie. Thirty yards of line were ripped from my reel as it made a run through an overhanging tree on the opposite bank. A quarter of an hour and three runs later, it was ready for the net. Disaster again – it was too big for the net, which collapsed as Doug tried to lift the monster out. A mad scramble ensued and somehow it was on the bank. It weighed 22lb 8oz of leather carp – the biggest ever caught from Ashford's RMC. After officially weighing, and having photographs taken by the local press (who actually walked all the way to the swim after being contacted by the club), the magnificent fish was returned to the water. I have won many prizes and accolades for this fish, but nothing comes close to the sense of achievement and self-satisfaction that I feel myself.

They were the words that I felt and wrote at the time. Surely the marriage was born out of the love affair with this wonderful water. On reflection, that night was to remain one of the most action-packed sessions I was ever to have at the canal. The rest of the

Bill Phillips' first ever twenty, of 22lb 8oz, taken from the Badger Sett on 18 June 1973.

season, although eventful in many, many ways, only produced a further three carp in 250 hours. But I never stopped enjoying the magic or the challenge. I had other, easier waters to fish but rarely betrayed the water I had grown so fond of.

From my diaries, a few memorable events involved the canal's wildlife more than the fish. Truly, in the early days, carp fishing was about much more than just catching carp. Only things that are rare or hard to

achieve have any real value, and that, I'm sure, was the driving force. Badgers and foxes became friends. Encounters were often startling to say the least. My diary reads: 'Almost kissed a fox. Don't know who had the biggest fright, me or the fox.'

Picture this: it was a warm and still August night in 1974. I was fishing alone in the big double. I doubt if there were any other anglers on the whole canal, as night fishing was rarely considered by the vast majority, early morning being the favourite. There was an eerie feel to the night air. It was very dark and felt stormy. The roof of the dugout had fallen in earlier in the season, so the brolly was erected to form a roof, which was just above the top of the bank. I could clearly hear the roar of the lions from the wildlife park on the hill to the north. I was never scared exactly, but would often feel uneasy, sort of goose-bumpy, with rising hairs on the back of my neck, as was the case on this night. I lay back in my deckchair, watching the bottle top indicators in the flickering candlelight. The session had been brilliant, producing two beautiful commons during the evening, 6lb 14oz and 9lb. A super result for me, encouraging dozing and fantasies of what was to come. Then, almost in slow motion, the brolly started to turn. There was virtually no sound as it continued to sway around. I absolutely froze, too frightened to move or look. God knows what I thought it was, but I do know I nearly gave birth. After what seemed an age, I found the courage to turn and look. By this time, the brolly was well on the tilt. My head was about level with the top of the bank and, as I peered over the edge of the dugout, I literally came nose to nose with the culprit. We both momentarily stopped and stared into each other's eyes and then all hell let loose. I jumped up, letting out a startled cry, knocking the brolly, rods, chair, candle and everything else flying. The fox gave a high-pitched yelp, and almost did a wheel spin as it bolted off and actually kicked dirt in my face. There I was, heart thumping, shaking and at the same time laughing at how ridiculous it must have looked. The remainder of the night was blank and uneventful but, every time I thought about it, I let out a chuckle. If anyone had been around, they would have thought I was tuppence short of a shilling.

One hot summer evening, when I was stalking with bunches of maggots and a bubble float – the little clear bubbles of plastic that could be partly filled with water for weight – there were a number of blue torpedo shapes drifting in and out of the margin lilies and basking, inaccessible, in the warm evening sun. Having spotted a possible target, I gently started an underarm swing in preparation for a gentle cast to the edge of the lilies. As the baited hook swung to and fro over the lily pads, there was a sudden wrench on the rod as it hooped over into its fighting curve. Christ! They must want them maggots really badly to leap out of the water for them, was my thought. But what a strange fight – no screaming run as would be the norm. No, just a thumping. Then I saw it, the biggest, fattest, greenest frog I had ever seen. Truly, it was the size of a tea plate. The only explanation was that it saw the maggots fly over its head, thought 'Big juicy fly', and went for it. What a caper getting it off the hook. Again, I was glad there was no one to see me wrestling with the damn thing, trying to let it go without hurting it. Eventually, it swam off, none the worse for its ordeal.

In 1974/75, a family of badgers took up residence in the big double swim and really made a mess of it. They became a part of every fishing session on the canal and belong as much in my memory as the carp themselves. Over the years, they often startled me, spooked the fish, always fascinated me and eventually became less shy, sometimes even taking bits of sandwiches and bait. I don't know how long badgers live, but they seemed to go through a couple of generations during the ten years or so that I knew them. They could, at times, be fairly aggressive. My poor old dog, Patches, a fishing companion in the later years, was absolutely petrified of them. When he heard them snorting about at night he would hide under my chair, shaking like a leaf. Whether it is the same family or not, I don't know, but certainly the Badger Sett, as the swim became known, is still there and very much alive. Long may they escape the call for a cull for they are magnificent creatures.

I could go on about the canal's wildlife, but I guess that I had better return to fishing. Or is it one and the same thing? By the end of the 1975 season I had spent six seasons and some 2,000-odd hours on the canal in pursuit of its carp. In my most successful year, 1974, I recorded a total of nine fish to 25lb 7oz. I wanted to be more successful from fewer hours, so that I could spend some time on other waters that were available to me, some of which held many and large carp. The RMC was certainly a difficult water, which I do believe was one of the big attractions, but also caused much pain.

I had, by this time, concentrated my RMC efforts on the two to three miles between West Hythe Dam and Aldergate Bridge, almost without exclusion. Again, this stretch was to be targeted for the 1976 season. A comprehensive baiting programme was to be followed by an opening week or two of fast and furious carp catching, thus satisfying my desires and allowing me to move on to some new water. Wrong! The super baiting programme started with the purchase of a small motorbike to make the twenty-two-mile round trip more bearable for my limited income. A couple of roving visits in April 1975 and I had located some fish, four commons to be exact, all around the 8lb mark. This was enough to induce the start of my baiting. The question was, with what? Past experience had proved potato and cereal-type baits to be very slow, with lots of tench and bream problems.

High-protein specials and exotics had produced a few carp and 550,000 eels (well, a lot anyway), and corn, nothing but tench and bream. I eventually decided that a biggish particle would serve as a bottom bait and a PYM floater would simply slaughter any surface fish whilst fooling the eels.

By 15 April, I had purchased a dozen cases of broad beans and made twelve pounds of dry mix (PYM), the eggs to be purchased weekly. The first loaf of floater was baked and I was away. One 5oz loaf and 30oz of particle every other day in the area where I had seen, and continued to see, fish in numbers of up to six at a time was the plan. Test lines were laid at fairly regular intervals and satisfaction gained in finding them stripped of bait almost every time after the first couple of weeks. These baits, incidentally, were only knotted on. By early May, hopes were high as, on most visits, carp were seen to be taking both top and bottom baits, although the tench were a little more than just interested. But you can't have it all your own way, I thought. Mid-May saw me digging out the bank to accommodate my bedchair and clearing three fingers in the lilies of the opposite margins, where my baits were to be placed. All looked great for the fantastic opening week I was sure I was going to have. Nearing the end of May, carp were still taking my baits. I had seen commons to around 16lb and a mirror of over 20lb.

Then things started to go wrong. As I watched after baiting, a long grey thing with a head like a greyhound sucked in one of the floaters. One out of the blue, thought I, but another went, and then another. The swim was alive with rotten, horrible eels. Yes, clooping eels mopping up my floater like pigs at a trough. The same thing happened on every visit. A 5oz loaf of floater was mopped up by eels coming up from seven feet of water. They took cubes of up to one and a half inches square, and even when I scattered brown and white crust cubes out among the floater, they were also taken, not so readily, but eventually they would all go apart from a few pieces of white crust that the carp shied away from. A problem, thought I. I remembered some advice on eel prevention given to me by the regional organizer of our friendly neighbourhood British Carp Study Group, which was to put some onion in the baits. That stops 'em, said he.

1976 – final swim preparation was done with long-handled shears.

At the time, I thought he was pulling my whatsit, but I had to try something, so onion it was. I started off with 5 per cent, and progressively increased until I was adding 20 per cent, but the eels continued to enjoy my precious floater.

Early June, and the eels were even bumping tench in the side if they tried to take the floater first. The carp seemed to have stopped taking it altogether, even when a piece did survive more than half an hour, so I decided to drop the floater and maybe just use a hook-bait on opening night, or use it for stalking with the hope that the eels may not find one odd piece so easily. The particle was going well and had been stepped up to 40oz a night. Final swim preparation was done by wading out with long-handled garden shears to trim the lilies exactly where I wanted. The Sunday afternoon strollers just didn't understand. They even laughed at me.

The fifteenth saw me set up by mid-afternoon and walking round to bait up. Three carp and about half a dozen tench were down on the bait immediately. How could I possibly fail? After what seemed like a lifetime's wait, midnight came. Two rods on a particle, one on floater and canal look out. At 00:10 I had a screaming run on the floater. Result? One smelly eel. Oh well, what was I to expect? Damn the floater and on with a spud. At 03:30, after a couple of tench, I was into a carp on particle. Another failure – confident carp plus particle equals throat teeth. I must admit, I was a little less than happy, especially as I didn't hook another carp until the end of the week, and felt like committing suicide when I lost one on the last morning of my stay after stalking it with floater. Damn thing spat the hook after getting snagged in the lilies for about ten minutes. Why didn't I go in? I don't know.

Nearly two months passed and, apart from one missed run on spud, I was achieving the unenviable feat of blanking a couple of times a week. On 18 August, a change of area to the Badger Sett looked like paying off when, on the second visit, after some light baiting with particle, a small common slid towards the net. Disaster again when, for some unknown reason, the hook shed and away swam my quarry. The very next evening saw a lower double common screaming line off my clutch and heading straight for the bough of a tree hanging in the water on the far bank. Somehow, the line tangled in that bough and would not free, although I could give and retrieve line. No way was I going to lose that fish, which was by then just lying exhausted in the snag. There was only one thing for it: down to my little red knickers, rod in the rests, net in teeth and away I went. I knew I should have learnt to swim, but after a few glugs and a bit of frantic doggy paddle, I made it. There I was, up to my ankles in mud, horrible slimy lilies hanging round me, water up to my shoulders and who knows what manner of nasties touching my person. That exhausted carp had, by this time, found a new lease of life and gone berserk, but I managed to grab the line and coax it into the lily-filled net. At last I had one; all I had to do was get to dry land. Then it happened; you just wouldn't credit it. The arms of the net broke and that precious fish casually swam away. How I got back to the bank I don't know, but I just lay there, half drowned, muttering rude words and wondering what I'd done to deserve such torture.

The next day was Friday. A long weekend must produce, I thought. But I was wrong again. Ill from the effects of my swim, I blanked again, the only event being a four-hour cat-and-mouse game with a twenty that just wouldn't play ball. A couple of weeks and several blanks later, another carp was lost on its initial run through the thick lilies, but somehow I kept going.

By mid-September my confidence was waning, no fish were seen and sessions tended to be fewer and shorter. On 18 September I was walking the canal to kill time before meeting a friend to fish another water. All I had with me was a rod, net and loaf. After an hour or so, a carp was spotted, rolling tight on the far bank. Crust and flake would not coax a take so I decided to find a worm to try, because the fish appeared to be feeding from an incoming flow caused by the recent heavy rain. With only freeline available, mud had to be moulded around the hook shank to enable a cast on to the far bank, so as not to splash and spook the fish. Wonders will never cease – it worked. A couple of tugs on the line and there it was – a nice, natural freelined worm in the opposite margins. A few seconds later, the carp was on; only a small common but it put up a great fight, and, needless to say, I treated that fish with the greatest respect all the way to the net. It weighed in at 9lb 4oz, but I was as pleased as I would have been with a twenty from any other water, probably more so. Why, I don't know, but to me that was my fish of the season. Not quite the slaughter I had planned, but a very satisfying fish.

Believe it or not, in the midst of all that, I did manage to take a few carp from some other waters and, apart from nearly being divorced, the kids calling me Uncle, a bank overdraft and demotion in my job, it was the most enjoyable season of misery I had ever had. Talk about inflation, take a look at the price of RMC carp:

Statistics

		Cost
Miles travelled	1,364	£34.10
Hours spent fishing (£2/hr in lost wages)	400	£800
Tackle depreciation		£20
Particle bait	336 tins	£28
PYM dry mix	12lb	£17
Eggs	228	£8.50
Worms	1	No charge
Total		£907.60

Carp caught: 1 at 9lb 4oz
Cost of carp: £6.13 per ounce
Mental state of angler: In question

The capture of that 9lb 4oz common was to be a turning point in my canal fishing. A maturity in my carp fishing methods and attitudes, especially on this type of water, came about as a result of that crazy 1976 season. I still had an inbred passion to catch Royal Military Canal carp but, due to a few problems on other waters, the object had to be achieved in fewer hours. My aim was to catch at least one RMC carp every season, but without using up too many valuable fishing hours. I reasoned that if hundreds of static rod hours resulted in blanks, and a short session (at least half of which was spent searching for fish) resulted in success, I should in theory be able to catch carp in far fewer hours by the use of thorough observation. This method of fishing is well known, but it is very difficult to resist wetting a line until fish are found. If they are not, to go home is not easy.

Observation fishing on the Royal Military Canal certainly paid dividends. In the 1977 season, observation plus only twenty-five hours' fishing resulted in the capture of one RMC carp. When compared with the 400 hours spent catching one carp in 1976, the improvement in both enjoyment and results was obvious.

There were also many added bonuses to this method of fishing: the thorough enjoyment of creeping along the banks observing not only the carp but many varied wild creatures, undisturbed in their natural environment. I have had the pleasure of watching such natural beauties as kingfishers skilfully diving for food and returning to small holes in the bank, where they then disappear only to pop out again and repeat the exercise. I would assume them to be rearing a new generation of those fluorescent gems. Wild mink, mistaken by many for otters, were often seen playing in family groups, their agility in the water a marvel to watch. Although I have only ever actually seen one catch an eel, I would suspect that they may well be responsible for many a fish capture. Herons and grebes slide long eels down their necks and, on one rare occasion, in the winter, I saw a bittern, its beak pointing to the sky in a disguise stance. Oh yes, the beauties of the water and its surrounding life are many and varied; the observant angler can enjoy them all.

My approach to the Royal Military Canal for the 1978 season was to be the same – observation first, and only if fish were found would a line be cast. A number of close season visits resulted in the location of only a few small commons. I therefore decided not to fish the RMC during the early part of the season, but would try to spend at least half a dozen evenings a month attempting to find one or two of the better fish. During each visit, a few Robin Red flavour baits would be put into the most likely holding areas in order to educate the carp. Although I carried on searching throughout the summer, no fish of any size were seen. Visits were made on selected days depending on the weather, and with reasonable regularity. Bait was not always introduced. As autumn drew close, I must confess that my confidence was waning.

Mid-October, and a couple of fair-sized carp were located. Then and only then did I wet a line for a couple of short blank sessions. It was a glorious late October, the water becoming very clear, the thick lily growth dying off and carp becoming much easier to locate. Baits were again introduced in small amounts and at last some apparently catchable carp were found. October 28 saw me creeping the banks on a beautiful warm and sunny afternoon. My armoury consisted of a 10ft soft rod and a 14lb BS line to combat the decaying weed and fallen tree branches, rod rest, landing net, a sack (just in case I caught a fish), bread crusts and some balls of soft paste, as previously introduced. After about an hour, and a walk of a mile or so, I found a big mirror rolling around in the margins. This fish looked ripe for catching on a piece of crust. I crawled through the bushes and watched for a while. What a fantastic sight it was too: clear water, a magnificent carp in full view, flaunting itself at me, picking at the odd leaf on the surface and thoroughly enjoying life. Very gently I presented a small piece of crust. After a few minutes the big fish swam close to the crust, stopped, flicked its fins, looked completely disgusted and swam away. That fish was undoubtedly disturbed by the presence of my crust.

Dragging my net from the bushes with some force, whilst trying to watch that departing carp, I set off in pursuit, but lost sight of it some hundred yards on. Consolation was found in the location of a very large common, which was grubbing about amongst the decaying vegetation in some three feet of gin-clear water. A small paste bait was flicked past the fish and then drawn back into its path. Unfortunately, whilst trying to gain the last few inches, my bait caught on a lily stem and fell off the hook. Unable to move a great deal, due to the proximity of the fish and the awkward position I had got into, it was not possible to rebait. Before I could decide on a plan of action, the fish moved to my hookless bait, dipped, sucked it in, paused for a second and swam away in the same direction as the mirror had done earlier.

I was by this time somewhat annoyed, with two good chances blown. But I did find some consolation in the knowledge that at least one fish was prepared to accept my bait on that particular day. All I had to do was find it again, or perhaps another, and present the bait in the same way. After a while, I found a group of four small commons happily grubbing the bottom, very close in at a depth of no more than two feet. A very rare sight indeed. Belly crawling close to them, I was able to present a bait by

A carp weighing 25lb 7oz in 1974.

casting and drawing back. The rod was gently placed in the rest with an indicator hanging at the butt. The reason for the indicator was that I could see the fish from my low-level position but not the bait. The fish gradually faded away. I had taken a great deal of care not to frighten them, but as so often happens they were aware of my presence and departed. Eager not to waste too much time fishing a barren patch, I clambered up into a bush and peered into the water. My bait was visible, but no fish. Evening was drawing near, the sun was beginning to retreat like a burnt-out fireball, and my hopes were wearing thin. On what was most likely my best ever spotting day on the Royal Military Canal, I looked like drawing a blank.

I clung uncomfortably to the bush, thinking of starting to work my way back to the van, which was by now a mile and a half away, and generally feeling sorry for myself. I mentally relived my chances of the big mirror and common, but in imagination I succeeded. Suddenly, out of the corner of my eye, I saw a dark shadow moving in the water. A very big fish, maybe the mirror seen earlier, and what's more it was moving towards the position of my bait. The feeling of excitement was tremendous. I knew that fish was going to get itself caught. My whole body was trembling as I slid back down to my rod and, not daring to breathe, settled to await events. Almost immediately, the

Four years later, in 1978, the same fish was caught at 32lb.

indicator twitched. An instant strike, and all hell was let loose. The situation was close to chaotic. I held hard to prevent the fish from reaching a fallen tree branch some twenty yards to my right. Not an especially dramatic fight, just bloody awkward due to my position; the bank and the half rotted lilies all tangled the line, surging through the water like something out of Jaws. Within a few minutes a massive mirror was wallowing on the surface. I pushed my net into the thicket of decaying vegetation and one of the net arms broke clean off. I think the argument with the bramble bush earlier may have been to blame. I used to break at least two nets every year, very often at criti-

cal times. Good carp tackle was less available then than it is now.

Anyway, there I was, a big hunk of lunging carp waiting to be netted and a broken net lying useless at my feet. I felt sick. Somehow I managed to wade in up to my knees, laid the net beside me using one hand as a spreader block, and dragged the fish over it. In one frantic move I dropped the rod, grabbed the net and lifted. Lifting that magnificent mirror up the bank was the most satisfying moment of my life. I stood there soaking wet and trembling with excitement as I gazed down at it. 'God, it's big!' I gasped, as I realized that it must be approaching thirty.

The two- or three-mile round trip to get some scales from the van seemed to be the longest journey ever. As I ran, I was panting to myself, 'Is it thirty? It's got to be thirty. No it can't be, not from the RMC.' Eventually, I got back with the scales and another sack, to give me the safety of double sacking my prize. The Avons hit the stop and I knew then that I had achieved more than my burning ambition of a thirty – I had achieved it on my water and with a new fish; in those days a very big fish indeed. It was later photographed and officially weighed at 32lb. I kissed it lovingly and returned it to the water. As that magnificent hunk of carp flicked its tail and disappeared, a peculiar shiver came over me. I could feel a sore dampness in my eyes – not sadness but sheer ecstasy. Not only a thirty, but from the RMC. Next was to be that common!

Contributory factors to the capture of that fish included good observation, patience, experience, luck and just rewards for the problems endured over the years of obsession, during which I had learnt so much from the water I loved. My fishing on the RMC for the next couple of years was largely focused on the common that I had seen take the hookless bait. I can now reveal that it was big, very big, possibly upper thirties or . . . However, I was only to see it a few more times, never having another opportunity to offer a bait.

In 1981, I was seconded to Nigeria for nearly a year. Shortly after my return, I moved from Kent to Wiltshire. My visits to the RMC became fewer and fewer. I still return and walk its banks occasionally, and even now it still stirs up my emotions, but I rarely fish. The sadness I feel is partly due to the loss of an era that can never be repeated on the canal, or anywhere else for that matter. Also, it is because my beloved water has fallen into some degree of disrepair. Ashford Club no longer has control, and the splitting up of sections controlled by a number of different organiza-tions has meant that it no longer receives the level of maintenance that Ashford and Cinque Ports applied when they were in control.

My total results from a decade of fishing the RMC are shown at the end of this chapter. I am sure that most people will be amazed at how few carp were caught over such a long period of time. True, but I remember every one in epic detail and worked like crazy on my own and against the odds. During that period, I only knew of a handful of other carp being caught from the notoriously difficult Ashford Angling Club stretch. However, during the same period two excellent and very successful carp anglers were catching far more than I from the Cinque Ports West Hythe area. They were Bob MacGregor and Tim Marshal, the only other true RMC carp pioneers I know. We always had a form of friendly rivalry. They caught many more fish than I did, including a lot of twenties, but my ace was the first thirty-pounder.

During that decade on the canal, I did, of course, fish other waters, and indeed was relatively successful. But none of the fish-catching experiences even came close to the sheer magic of the canal: the mystery, solitude, challenge, the beauty of the water and its surroundings, and the fish themselves. Certainly to me, the number of doubles is not a measure of either ability or enjoyment; memories are. If a capture is etched in your memory, it is probably truly worthy and not belittled by hundreds of others. The more difficult a thing is to achieve, the greater the value it holds. In Chapter 11 you will read how modern angling techniques and abilities have well and truly exposed the potential of the West Hythe sections. However, I really do believe that the key to the Iden to West Hythe section has still to be found by whoever has the determination to try to unlock its secrets. If you consider that its fifteen-mile length represents thirty miles of margins, that is effectively one hell of a big lake. So find them first – much more of a priority than on any other type of water – because you can't easily cast to them if they are even as little as fifty yards away. Observation plus stealth, patience and determination will equal success.

Year	Carp caught	Largest	Hours Fishing	Hours preparing and observing
1970	nil	nil	200	20
1971	nil	nil	220	40
1972	nil	nil	250	50
1973	5	22lb 8oz	250	100
1974	9	25lb 7oz	500	100
1975	2	8lb 9oz	280	125
1976	1	9lb 4oz	400	300
1977	1	8lb 14oz	25	150
1978	1	32lb	20	200
1979	4	26lb 3oz	70	120
1980	2	9lb	12	100
Total	25		2,227	1,305

Total hours fishing and preparing = 3,532

11 The Royal Military Canal

Steve and Rich Howkins

Perhaps uniquely amongst the carp waters of the UK, the Royal Military Canal was constructed as a fortification against foreign invaders. Completed in 1806, after the threat of Napoleon's armies had gone, the canal was designed to provide a defensive position along the flatlands of the Romney Marsh, from Seabrook in the east to Rye, twenty-two miles to the west.

Today, the canal has a multitude of uses, both agricultural and recreational; indeed the nature of the waterway varies dramatically along its length. From its confluence with the Eastern Rother at Iden Lock to West Hythe, it passes through mainly agricultural land where the primary functions are land drainage and irrigation. Past West Hythe the surroundings become more urban, and as such the agricultural burden diminishes. The canal is divided into sections by sluice dams at Appledore and Lympne. The three sections, although connected in name, are each very different waters as fish stocks are unable to move from one section to another.

The canal has contained carp since before the last war, but only since the mid- to late-sixties has it attracted the attention of local carp anglers. Although the mainstay of the fishery is double-figure fish, the water began producing 20lb fish in the late sixties and the first thirty-pounder in 1978, so the big fish potential is beyond question.

Unfortunately, most of the canal is leased by the Environment Agency to local clubs on a three-yearly basis, so a consistent stocking policy to replace the monsters of the past is never viable. The one exception to this state of affairs is on the eastern section, from Lympne Dam to Seabrook Sluice, where one club has had control for a great many years. This section has seen the bulk of the carp angling pressure over the last quarter of a century, and has produced a great deal of fish, both large and small. Indeed, it is almost certainly the most densely populated section along the canal's length, this statistic being only relative with little more than 100 carp within five miles of waterway.

Living very close to the canal, we have fished this section extensively and draw most of our experiences from it. The topography of the stretch is very different from the rest of the fishery; its agricultural and drainage burden is minimized, and as a consequence the water is shallower and more silty. Fortunately, trees and bushes thrive along both banks where they would otherwise interfere. The surroundings contrast sharply with other sections. Gone are the flat windswept fields of the Romney Marsh; the canal here follows the Saxon Shore Way at the foot of a steep escarpment, and flows past housing estates, factories, through a busy town, skirting a golf links, before reaching the sea at Seabrook Sluice. Access along this length is simplified by its proximity to the main coastal trunk road.

This section has always received at least 95 per cent of the angling pressure, and as such the possibilities of uncaught biggies are negligible. But large fish remain from previous stockings, and thanks to the foresight of the controlling club new fish are

Richard Howkins with a 20lb+ winter leather carp, part of a short-session 20lb brace.

breaking the 20lb barrier as we write. We have carp fished this section for over ten years and watched them for many years before that. What we have observed in this time has, we feel, made us better anglers and enabled us to acquire experience which we have put to use when fishing other waters, particularly large gravel pits and rivers.

The crux of fishing rivers, drains and canals is that you are fishing a small water within a much larger one, meaning that technically you are always in a close range situation within a water, where the nearest fish may be several miles away. A pessimist may suggest that these waters hold the location problems of large waters (walking and looking), coupled with the problems of margin fishing (keeping quiet). The optimist, however, would see that once located, provided basic fishing lore is followed, the

fish can be quite easily caught. Judging by the amount of carp anglers fishing our moving waters it is pleasing to see how many pessimists are happy on their landlocked puddles, leaving the good fish to the good anglers.

The carp along the canal can be observed and their behaviour monitored readily on their favoured stretches as we attempt to understand them. Much of the behaviour we observe is routine and their appearance in certain stretches at certain times of the year is as predictable as if they were programmed. This is particularly true of the Hythe town stretch, where each May the entire population gathers to spawn and to feast upon the bread thrown in by local residents for the ducks. On 16 June though ...

Elsewhere on the canal, where local legend has it that a flying bomb landed during the last war, good numbers of fish gather each winter in a twelve-foot deep hole. This spot is particularly hot during low water conditions, as the rest of the canal at that point barely exceeds three feet in depth, the only snag being beating the pike anglers to the spot in the morning.

Each individual fish has its own character and preferences, with some being gregarious, others shy, some stupid and some seemingly intelligent, but all of their observed behaviour helps to build a bigger picture of how the population of carp behave, which as mentioned earlier has given us immense benefit when we

Steve Howkins landing a common carp on the Royal Military Canal.

approach other waters. At times the fishing is simple and a number of fish can be caught, but at the other end of the scale they can behave as neurotically as those in land-locked puddles. What is interesting is that during the difficult periods that normally occur during high summer and deep winter, fish can be quite easily tempted to feed, but there exists a fine line between success and failure that is rarely crossed during scratching time. We have found that during such periods, and indeed at any other time, catches can be enhanced through a concerted prebaiting campaign in order to win the fish's confidence. After several evenings' baiting, the carp's defences are often lowered to such an extent that several may be taken in a session, usually within a short time.

This brings us to the actual approach we favour when fishing this water. Basically, we like to locate the areas where we judge or have seen fish to be present. Several light baitings to gain favour with them are followed by a number of short sessions equipped with the minimum amount of tackle. Two or three rods, net, bag and seat are all that is needed to catch a carp or two. We rarely stay longer than three hours in one spot, as once fish are caught or are aware of our presence, the shallow nature of the fishery ensures that the fish do not hang around for long. The fishing is conducted in a similar manner to the way in which a roving river angler would fish for barbel and chub: a few baits are scattered in likely looking swims, with up to half a dozen swims fished in a morning. This opportunist approach is a very interesting and rewarding style. One of our best catches fell in this manner when Rich landed five in one morning from three different swims. Two swims fished the next day produced four more carp, including a twenty-plus common.

As far as location is concerned, certain areas are tenanted by carp throughout the entire year, yet other stretches remain completely barren, save for the odd fish passing through. We're sure that all location pointers will be described in depth elsewhere within this book so we won't elaborate here; however, it is noticeable that fish favour particular features to the exclusion of other equally inviting spots nearby. Each year they will return to certain overhanging bushes or a certain set of moored boats, when other similar places are rarely visited. With experience it is possible to judge when fish are inhabiting these areas without an actual visual sighting – coloured water, bubbles, or even more bizarre a group of alarmed-looking whirlygig beetles are all

Muddy conditions in January at the Royal Military Canal.

reliable clues as to the carp's whereabouts.

Physical sightings of the fish are obviously the most beneficial indicators as their numbers, size and mood can be quickly assessed. At times no fish can be spotted for miles, yet on other days every spot seems to hold a couple. During periods of heavy rain the canal will colour up and the water level will rise accordingly. Although a visual sighting is nigh on impossible at these times, these happen to be our favourite conditions, particularly in winter, as the fish seem more willing to feed. Instinct and experience come to the fore when locating fish, and some of our best catches have occurred after heavy and prolonged rainfall when the water is high and dirty.

The fish themselves are great travellers, often moving several miles in one day. Indeed, the fish themselves are often vulnerable to capture after a long distance swim. Recognized fish have often been seen or caught in one area, only to be caught within a very short space of time a few miles away. A large known fish that we captured one morning was observed swimming quickly away from the area in one direction, only to be spotted happily taking floaters, in a catchable state, two miles the other way the next morning. Whether this is because of the need to replace lost energy or because their defences are lowered in territory they are unfamiliar with is pure speculation, but it is a point worth bearing in mind when fishing large waters.

Several summers ago a road bridge had to be replaced across the canal which necessitated damming a 100-yard section and draining the water between. To maintain water levels on both sides of the site an 18in pipe was laid connecting each section. That summer at least two carp made the perilous journey through the pipe as they were captured on both sides! Another interesting pattern we have observed is a pecking order within the population, where the larger fish are the leaders. As an illustration, when the

Richard Howkins with a 20lb+ carp.

largest known fish is captured it invariably leads to all the other carp vacating that area for many weeks – something that rarely occurs when numbers of modest fish are taken from one swim.

One of the most popular areas on the canal is the Hythe town section. Access is easy along this length, but it also happens to be as far removed from anybody's image of a carp water as possible, which of course adds to the enjoyment. Sessions here nearly always involve boaters, ducks, noisy kids, noisy traffic and drunks, in no particular order of preference. As long as you accept this then good fishing can be enjoyed in the most unlikely situations.

When a fish is being played and landed crowds usually gather, and comments such as 'Ooh I never knew they grew that big', or more commonly, 'What's that? A cod?' are rife. Some of the best descriptions have fallen to the spawning fish in May, which have been labelled as 'sharks' and 'seals'. A friend was once reported to the local copper for 'Drowning dogs in big black sacks'. Taken in the correct spirit this is all good fun. Instant hero status can be achieved by catching and returning a good double whilst declaring it was 'only a tiddler'.

Another section borders a housing estate which brought problems of a different kind to a friend one evening. A carp had taken up

Steve Howkins with a 30lb mirror.

residence under a particular overhanging tree on the far bank. A freelined floater was cast repeatedly at the fish, with the cast falling short each time and our friend getting more frustrated by the second.

'This time!' he told us as he prepared his next cast.

Unfortunately, 'that time' resulted in his bait becoming firmly lodged in the branches of the aforementioned tree. After a swift tug-of-war the bait came free like a bullet out of a gun, flew over our heads, over the hedge behind us and into an apple tree in someone's back garden. Without giving it a moment's thought our friend reeled in the slack and continued to pull, only this time even harder. What the lady in the garden thought as her prize tree doubled over on a calm summer evening can only be guessed at (she couldn't see us from behind the

hedge), but her squeals of horror when she saw what was happening saw us running down the bank like kids once the line had come free and we had stopped laughing.

Our experiences have helped tremendously with our all-round angling as we have been able to use what we have observed when fishing other waters. The carp of the Royal Military Canal are great teachers and we are sure they will continue to confuse, entertain and baffle us in the future. Carp fishing will continue for years to come, indeed the fishery produced an unknown 25lb-plus common only last year, and young fish are reaching similar weights along the Cinque Ports Angling Society section in Hythe. Unfortunately, the number of known large fish from stockings in the fifties and sixties is alarmingly small, and it is doubtful that any uncaught contemporaries exist even in the more remote and less fished stretches. However, canal carping will never be number orientated, which in itself is a blessing.

We hope we have given an insight into this interesting fishery, and to canal fishing in general. There is probably little we can add here on the technical side that isn't covered elsewhere within this book. The basics of carp fishing remain unaltered whether an angler fishes canal, river or pit. However, canals and rivers provide the thinking angler with the space in which to pursue his sport, which is uncommon these days. Many anglers cannot come to terms with the long walks, the isolation and the lack of space for a dome – this is to our benefit.

12 The River Nene: A Cut Above the Rest

Dave Phillips

Back in the 1960s, the River Nene was the talk of the carping world. To be precise, it was one insignificant little backwater off the main river at Peterborough that was causing all the fuss: the Electricity Cut. Hardly a name to conjure up dreams of mist-heavy lakes, girded by flag irises and meadowsweet. Locations such as the Pools, Redmire and Ashlea were top of the class in mystery, magic and mythical monsters. The Electricity Cut was the boy who sat at the back of the class and picked his nose.

But that mattered not a jot to the carping pioneers of the day, who believed that their favoured species went into hibernation on 1 November, setting their alarm clocks for 16 June. It was supposed that no self-respecting carp would deign to feed during the rigours of a British winter, so most carpers packed away floppy Mark IVs, hung up their split-cane hats, and roasted their nuts in front of crackling log fires as they sharpened their shortened salmon hooks and thought long and hard about which varieties of potatoes they would grow on their allotments to parboil in preparation for the glorious 16th.

For the benefit of younger readers, I must explain at this point that the above is a reference to the days when there used to be a close season and you couldn't wet a line between 14 March and 16 June. However, nobody has yet explained why 16 June was ever described as glorious. Every angler over the age of thirty knows that it was inevitably cold, miserable and pissing down with rain – the day on which the dreams of the previous months rapidly turned to blank nightmares.

Okay, I know this is starting to sound like a history lesson, but in this instance history can be exciting, because this is a long-winded way of telling you about the origins of river carp fishing, and why every boilie-slinger who's not a peg short of a full bivvy should save a fortune in syndicate fees and go messing about on the river. You've already invested in this book, so the idea is to get the most out of it.

Back to the Electricity Cut. In the free-lined, potato-swinging sixties it was a short canal that ran from the coal-fired power station that supplied Peterborough with electricity, to the River Nene. It was designed to shift warm water from the cooling towers to the river.

In the sub-zero depths of winter it steamed so thick you'd be hard-pressed to find it, but once you'd fought your way through the industrial smog you found yourself on the muddy, worn and litter-strewn banks of the carp water from hell. It was a place where you had to cast your bait out quick before a rat the size of a cat snatched it in mid-air. If you didn't have to clear a pile of rubbish from your swim, you knew you'd chosen a duff peg. But the rewards were there.

Back in 1948, when carp were considered an exotic species in British waters, the forward-thinking local river board had boosted the Nene with the same strain of carp as had been stocked into Redmire Pool. They were only fingerlings, and could all have been snapped up by the river's notorious stock of small but abundant pike, but some obviously survived. Just eleven years later, in 1959, the Nene produced its first 20lb-plus carp – a specimen that topped the magic mark by 6oz and was landed by Peterborough angler Don Barnes. It came from the Electricity Cut.

Now, a fish of that size today will bring a smile to the captor's face but hardly raise an eyebrow elsewhere. Four decades ago, things were very different – a 20lb carp would make headline news in the *Angling Times*, launched just a few years earlier. By coincidence, *AT*'s headquarters were in Peterborough, just a mile from the Electricity Cut, ensuring that the venue got maximum publicity over the next decade as its fame spread. The Cut, as it was known locally, was – and still is – situated on River Lane in the city. It was only a quarter of a mile long, but on freezing cold winter nights carp enthusiasts from all over the county congregated to fish shoulder to shoulder along its entire length.

By 1964, Grantham angler Stan Hill had recorded the Cut's first carp to top the 30lb mark, weighing in at 31lb 12oz. Two months later, local teenager Peter Harvey added a 33lb 12oz beauty, which was caught at the same weight within weeks by Londoner Peter Hemingway.

All these big fish were caught in the depths of winter, usually at night and mainly on the fashionable bait of the day, namely those parboiled potatoes which were free-lined in the margins of the cut. Others were caught on bread, including floating crust suspended below the rod tip.

However, another Londoner, William Beta, bucked the nocturnal and winter trends on opening day of the 1965 season when he fished cheese in broad daylight and landed the biggest carp of all at 34lb 4oz. It was Britain's record river carp at the time and still stands as an official Nene record today, although much bigger fish are rumoured to have been landed by specialists anxious to avoid publicity, including a 38lb monster from the featureless North Bank match stretch below Peterborough.

In retrospect, that short run of thirty-pounders was in all likelihood one and the same fish. Certainly, some of the Cut's winter residents were repeat captures, despite the crude tactics of the day. One 20lb-plus specimen that was caught repeatedly was known as 'Lumpy' on account of its deformed mouth. At the time, there was some debate about whether it was an 'easy' capture because it had suffered some form of brain damage, but in those days 'mug' fish were unknown and the only reason the unfortunate Lumpy was registered as a repeat was because it was so easily recognizable.

In those days, winter carping pioneers on the Cut included some famous names, such as Jim Gibbinson, then based in Northampton, and his sparring partner Fred Wagstafle, who was later to achieve lasting fame as a pioneering piker before switching his attention to reservoir trout with devastating effect. On 1 January 1966, a young Peterborough angler, Elliott Smith (later Symak) landed a 22lb carp from the Cut that was the first of seven over 20lb he caught whilst fishing with a local student, David Moore. The duo's catches dominated the winter scene on the venue until 1970, when the power station closed and the hot water ceased to pour in. Interest in the Cut subsequently disappeared, but those two anglers certainly didn't. Elliott became a big-name carper in the seventies and went on to become a noted fishery owner, whilst David became recreation development officer for Anglian Water, controlling the prestigious trout fisheries of Rutland Water, Grafham Water, Pitsford and Ravensthorpe.

Ironically, my own introduction to the River Nene and its carp came during that period. I was eleven years old at the time

The first fish of the new season – a 25lb 2oz carp from the River Arun.

Andy Sloane with a linear mirror from the River Avon.

The Royalty Fishery on the River Avon.

Neil Wayte and a 21lb 8oz winter common carp from the Avon.

Gary Dennis and a typical Lincolnshre fens common.

Below   *Ted Head with a Suffolk Stour common of 24lb at Brundon Mill.*

Rob Ness and Gary Peet with two 25lb+ commons from the River Medway.

Steve Howkins and a 20lb floater-caught mirror from the Royal Military Canal.

Dave Passmore with a 22lb opening night mirror from the Rother.

Terry Brookes with the River Soar record, a 25lb 3oz mirror.

Terry Brookes with a common caught from the nearside margin.

Shaun Harrison's River Trent set-up.

Shaun Harrison with a good Trent mirror.

Charles Wilson and a 14lb 4oz fish from the River Weaver.

Shaun McSpadden and a River Weaver common.

Keith Blakey with a good winter canal carp, an 18lb mirror.

and living thirty miles away in West Norfolk, but in September 1967 my dad and brother-in-law decided to attend a Peterborough United home match and gave me the choice of watching the Posh or going fishing. There was no contest, and while they endured ninety minutes of Fourth Division football, I sat a few hundred yards away on the Cut – the Wembley of winter carping. It wasn't winter, of course, and I wasn't carp fishing; like all eager youngsters I was swapping baits and untangling lines with fellow angling apprentices. Until that day, my early endeavours with lobworm baits had accounted for plenty of Fenland eels and perch, but a few borrowed maggots saw me swing in my first ever roach, rudd and bleak – the latter an exotic species I hadn't even heard of. Even better, one of my new-found friends eventually caught a freshly-minted mirror carp of all of 2oz. It was the first carp I'd ever seen, but even all these years later I can remember that it fought differently to the other little fish we caught that day. It put up a sterling scrap of several seconds before finally lying at rest in its proud captor's palm. There and then I vowed to catch a Nene carp myself. If I'd known it would take nearly thirty years I'd probably have given up fishing in favour of football.

Fast forward now. After many, many years of wanderings that have got nothing at all to do with this story, I finally pitched up in the early 1990s in East Northamptonshire, close to the River Nene. The proximity to the latter was entirely by accident rather than design, and although the river was literally on my doorstep I ignored it in favour of venues with more favourable pedigrees. Hence I travelled to Ireland for big, lure-caught pike, and to the River Welland for the chub that were my favourites of the time. It wasn't until 16 June 1994 – yet another opening day – that I finally found myself on the banks of the Nene after an abortive lure session on a local gravel pit. A

few days earlier I'd recorded my best ever plug-caught pike of 29lb 1oz and 26lb 1oz from an Irish lough, and the Nene valley only seemed to offer an anti-climax … until I turned up on a certain backwater of the river itself. That evening the carp were spawning in shallow water and I didn't even bother to throw out a plug for the pike, because I was so engrossed in watching the carp at close range.

To cut a long story short, I spent most of the rest of that summer shadowing those carp, many of which were clearly in excess of 20lb and, I suspected, some even over the 30lb mark. I was hooked… even if the carp weren't.

Slinging freelined flake at those nomadic monsters produced a few satisfying results, with carp into double figures, but it wasn't until later that summer, when I embarked on a planned campaign, that I finally got amongst the big ones. By that time my old mate Mark Williams had joined me, and we began baiting a lily-lined bay with maple peas to concentrate the roaming packs of carp and wean them on to a bait we could present on the hook.

That summer, an unseasonal storm briefly thwarted our plans. Heavy rain saw the river rise three feet overnight, and August was subsequently a wash-out. But although fishing was out of the question whilst the Nene was in spate, the bait went in regardless – several pounds of maple peas into the same swim at the same time every evening.

Eventually, the river fined down and the time came. Mark and I turned up at 3.30pm – an hour before the ritual baiting time – baited up and settled in. Very soon afterwards I had a screaming run to three maple peas threaded on to a hair rig and duly banked a pot-bellied common. Minutes later, Mark did battle with a 5lb-plus tench, which I photographed. Whilst I was doing so, I got another screaming run, but by the time I'd sprinted twenty yards back to my

Michelle Conway with a 19lb common from the River Nene.

swim it had reached the weed and shed the hook. Meanwhile, the sky had darkened drastically and a thunderstorm broke above us. It lashed down for several minutes before the clouds parted and the sun shone through. At that very moment I got another run.

At the time I was fishing 8lb line on 1.5lb test curve rods, but the fight was never in any doubt. Although the heavy fish I'd connected with put up dogged resistance, it came to the net fairly quickly. It turned out to be a scale-perfect common carp of exactly 28lb. The next session, I landed a 23lb 12oz mirror carp and, a day later, a common of 22lb-odd hit the net. The carp were in the swim, they were hungry, and we caught them – along with plenty of scrappy double-figure specimens that put their bulkier cousins to shame. Sorry, but it was as easy as that.

My smugness turned to frustration, however, in October that year, when the first frost of the autumn sent water temperatures plummeting ... and the carp dispersed throughout the river. With blanks suddenly becoming the norm, my sessions became fewer, although a handful of boilies thrown in as free offerings (as well as one on the hook) picked up the odd double when I took the occasional carp excursion as a break from the winter's piking. The following summer, I again headed for Ireland for pike, and continued lure fishing for predators through those long, hot months back in England. Even the Nene produced some scrapping double-figure snappers and I didn't bother with the carp again until one day in late summer when the heatwave finally broke and a warm, wet wind from the south-west appeared during the middle of a plugging session.

A 28lb common from the River Nene.

Suddenly, a sultry summer's day chilled as the sky greyed and choppy waves broke the oily calm of the sluggish river. Within minutes big carp began crashing on the surface. Soon, the whole river appeared to be dominated by big fish intent upon rolling, leaping or swirling on the top. I've never seen anything like it before or since, but as an opportunist angler I didn't need any further hints ... I headed straight for my local grain merchant and bought a sack of maples.

The baiting-up process began again, this time for a week, and along with the maples I added several kilos of readymade prototype boilies I'd been given by a bait manufacturer. Each evening, as I lobbed and catapulted the free offerings into the chosen pitch, I'd sit back and wait as the carp rolled and bubbled in the area. Success was guaranteed; it was only a case of choosing the day on which to slay 'em.

I was shaking with trepidation when I finally tackled up on the bank of that hallowed (and heavily-baited) swim. I knew the chances would come, but I didn't want to mess them up. I needn't have worried – within an hour I'd landed commons of 25lb 8oz, 19lb and 16lb. My girlfriend Michelle joined me the next day and banked the first carp she'd ever seen – another nineteen-pounder. I fished standard boilies on the bottom, popped 'em up and fished any manner of change baits. But boilies were best, because they scored with the carp; lesser baits like sweetcorn picked up nuisance bream, tench and roach. Those carp averaged 16lb apiece and 80 per cent of them were commons that looked as though they'd never been hooked before. Again, only the dank cloak of winter stopped the action and my own enthusiasm.

At ninety-odd miles long the River Nene is the biggest top-notch carp fishery in the country. I wouldn't dare to estimate the number of 20lb-plus fish that swim within its weedy depths, the majority of which are scale-perfect commons that have never seen the bankside. Thirty-pounders aren't out of the question either; I've suffered the frustration of seeing fish far bigger than I've ever caught feeding in the margins below my rod tip.

Today, the Electricity Cut at Peterborough is no more than another backwater off the main river that holds a carp or two. But the rest of the river is alive with the progeny of those early specimens that have, over the last three decades, spread out and colonized the entire watercourse between Northampton and the Dog in a Doublet tidal sluice below Peterborough. The Nene is sluggish and around seven feet deep on average. In summer the weed growth is lush and there are dense lilies along the margins and in the bays and dead arms. But there is always clear water in the middle of the river, caused by boat traffic. I have had my best results close to features, but in truth there are carp throughout. Repeat captures have shown that the fish can be very nomadic.

Parboiled potatoes apart, very simple baiting techniques will help you to get amongst them.

13 The River Rother

Neil Wayte and Dave Passmore

The River Rother rises near Mayfield in Sussex, and before reaching Robertsbridge, some fourteen miles downstream, it is joined by several upland tributary streams. Above Newenden, some seven miles further downstream, the Kent ditch joins the main river. Below Newenden the river is also joined by the Hexdon and New Mill Channels, before it continues on for a further twelve miles down to Rye. In total, the length of the river is some thirty-four miles.

The River Rother was once known for excellent chub, but when a dam was built to prevent flooding and help with the drainage of the surrounding farmland, the chub fishing declined. The river became more of a drain than a natural river, and these changes benefited bream, tench and of course carp. The carp had been present for many years; I remember speaking to an old float angler who said that he could remember catching carp back in the 1950s around Blackwall Bridge. I'm sure the stopping of the flow in the summers helped the carp to prosper.

At first glance the water authority's work produced a uniform and rather boring fishery, but a walk along the banks reveals plenty of features and fish-holding areas. The majority of visible features are in the margins on both sides of the river. In some stretches there are weedbeds on the marginal shelves, but for some reason these do not come up every year. Quite why this happens is not clear, but it does seem to be related to the amount of rainfall the previous winter. If the water authority is forced to run off the floodwater quickly, the roots of the weeds seem to be washed off the

shelves by the force of the extra water and take a couple of years to recover.

Also on the marginal shelves are odd beds of reeds which have sufficient depth of water around their stems for the carp to get into to feed and shelter. Last winter, when the water level had dropped by a couple of feet, I noticed that the roots of a weedbed had been exposed and were actually growing out of the bank rather than off the shallow shelf. Below the roots the bank was undercut, providing the carp with an excellent place to hide and feed. This spot will be baited next summer when the levels are higher, and I'm sure it will be a good spot to fish.

The third feature of the margins is any area where the bank drops straight into the water; these areas are often devoid of vegetation. With no shelf the water close in is deep and the carp can be caught inches from the bank.

I'm sure that the carp feed on any worms or grubs that are exposed below the water line. These are natural larders for the carp and any bait placed here will be taken. When fishing a river, most anglers either fish the far bank or down the middle of the river, which is fine, but ignore the nearside margin at your peril. Both Dave and I have caught plenty of carp from the nearside, either under the rod tip or with baits fished up or down the river in the near margin. The advantage of fishing the nearside is that you can place your baits accurately in holes in the weed or on the edge of it; placing the freebies is also a doddle.

The last features worth mentioning are the mouths of the drains that criss-cross the land surrounding the Rother. These vary in size from simple ditches to drains that are fisheries in their own right. The smaller ones can be ignored, but the larger ones that have concrete culverts built to hold their mechanical pumps and screens are holding areas. They are also possible feeding areas, but although carp have been seen jumping, I've not caught from the mouth. I have caught a few yards either side of them, however. Directly in front of the outlet the force of the water has scoured out the bottom of the river, exposing some clean gravel, and the silt that is disturbed builds up some way downstream. Either side of these humps is an excellent spot to fish because of the food build-up. It is also a good winter spot because it gives the carp something to hide behind when the river is flowing.

Now that we have moved on to the features in the middle of the river, it is fair to say that any form of snag on the bottom will hold fish; the bigger the snag, the more fish are likely to use it as a holding area. These features can be found by casting a lead along the river and pulling it back. You could use a marker float to give you the exact position of the snag, but this would prove expensive because of the number of marker floats that you would lose. A lead tied on the end of the line will in most cases pull through a lot of the snags, and if you mark the spot on the bank with a stick or marker you can then bait up in the general area of the snag. One swim that we have found has lots of tree stumps in the middle of the river and has proved to be the most consistent swim on the river. Dave has had two excellent opening days on this swim.

I would go as far as to say that the mid-river snags hold more of the carp than the weed- or reedbeds, and baited regularly will hold the widely travelling carp for longer than any of the marginal features. Fishing the weeds or reeds will give you the chance to catch fish as they move along the river. If you can find a swim with a snag in the middle and weeds in the margins then you have the best of both worlds.

This winter Dave spotted another way of finding mid-river snags that will be familiar to anglers whose rivers flow all of the time, but to us it only became evident as the river started to flow with the first of the winter rain. As the water flowed over the top of the snag the surface water boiled as it is pushed upwards. This allowed us to quickly find snags that we had not previously known about. When we started fishing the Rother, Dave and I spent a lot of time walking the banks to try to find the fish. Occasionally, we would see a fish in the weeds, but more often than not all we would see would be a bow wave as we spooked one. This would often have a domino effect as the spooked fish caused others to spook. You may think that this would ruin our fishing but it was mainly done in the close season so there was no damage done, and it gave us a good idea of the amount of fish in a certain stretch. It also gave us an idea of those areas that very rarely held fish so that we could concentrate on those in which we had seen fish more often. Walking the bank as often as possible, looking for fish, can cut down the amount of time spent fishing less sparsely populated areas.

Once you have found an area that you think contains some fish, the next thing is to prebait your swim. My first attempt at fishing for carp a couple of years previously had been unsuccessful because I didn't think that the carp would recognize boilies as a food source, so I baited heavily with sweetcorn and hemp and subsequently caught far more tench and bream than was good for my health. A local journalist and angler decided to try for carp on the Rother and baited under one of the bridges with boilies. He caught straight away, and when he told me I needed no further encouragement to have a go. At that time I had seen carp, so I had a talk with Dave and we spent the last month of the close season walking the banks of the river. Although we did not see many fish there was enough evidence of carp to convince us to prebait the stretch.

We spent three weeks prebaiting a stretch of maybe half a mile, and then as opening day got closer we decided on the two swims that we would fish. These were the only spots that we baited for the last week of the close season. Three weeks of prebaiting might not seem hard work, but the two spots we chose were one and a half miles from the nearest bridge. It took us twenty-five minutes to walk there, and thirty minutes to drive to the river, so just to get some bait into the river took at least two hours. We did this three nights a week, putting in a twelve-egg mix each time. This of course had to be rolled as well, so a bit of prebaiting added up to a lot of hard work. Perhaps you can now start to see that carp fishing on the rivers is not quite as easy as pulling up at your local lake for a weekend's fishing. But the more effort you put in, the more you will get out.

After our initial effort you will not be surprised to find out that when I walked up the river on opening night carrying all my gear, I was more than a little miffed to see two float anglers already set up in my swim. I had never seen them beforehand and I have never seen them again. I turned round and walked back to see Dave, who was fishing some seventy-five yards below. I very nearly carried on back to the van and probably would never have fished the river again. However, Dave had seen a couple of fish top at the bottom of the straight he was fishing, and tried very hard to convince me to stay and give it a go. Not only had he seen fish at the bottom of the straight, but he had fish showing all the time over his bait; it was all I could do to stop him casting out there and then and it was only 7 o'clock!

After a cup of tea I had calmed down enough to think about fishing. I really didn't fancy fishing an area that had not seen any bait during our prebaiting campaign,

but going on Dave's word I set up for the night some 200 yards downstream from him. I must say that my confidence was at rock bottom, but I had walked all the way up there so I decided to give it one night. I had nothing at all during the night, which was hard because just after midnight Dave shouted out for help and I netted an absolute cracker for him.

DAVE'S OPENING NIGHT

Being self-employed I had taken the Monday off work and had arrived at the river about midday to start the long walk up to my swim. Prior to the opening of the season I had baited three swims, not really knowing where I was going to start. I planned to spend the rest of the afternoon watching the river to see if the carp would show themselves and give me a clue as to which swim to settle into for the night. I left my gear in the first swim and continued up to where I had baited a longish straight that had one of the features mentioned earlier – a steep mud bank dropping into the river. After half an hour without seeing anything I noticed some other anglers turning up so I walked back to my tackle. They passed by where I had my tackle and settled down in the swim that Neil had prebaited. Of all the swims to pick on the river they picked that one, and of all the people to do it to it had to be Neil. Whilst I sat there wondering what would happen when Neil turned up, a carp leapt from the river right in front of me. It was a common of 15lb. That was it: decision made. I thought about what to do for about twenty seconds, and in went 2lb of bait right on the spot where the fish had jumped.

Two hours later and I had seen no sign of the fish; I thought that I had blown my chances by baiting up on its head. Fortunately, another fish showed tight to the far bank next to an old mooring post. It was definitely a different fish, another common, but bigger, maybe close to the magical 20lb mark. I decided that there were more fish there and that they had not been put off by the bait, so I put some more in, spreading it from bank to bank at an angle. I hoped that this would stop any fish moving up or down the river and hold these travelling fish in front of me. Neil and I sat drinking tea until it got dark and then Neil returned to his swim.

With just an hour or so to go until midnight I could see that it was a good fish. I had to follow it down towards Neil on its initial run, leaving the landing net behind in the swim. It was obvious that I was connected to a very powerful fish and I had to shout to Neil for help. By the time he arrived I had managed to get the fish under control and I was back in my swim. The fish was chugging up and down the margins under my feet, but it had not been back to

the surface since it rolled at the start of the fight. By this time I had told Neil that it was possibly a twenty, something that we both wanted to catch from the Rother. Neil netted it without any dramas and we carried the fish to the back of the swim and laid it on the unhooking mat amongst the long grass. Neil was already saying that I was a jammy so and so and that he reckoned it was well over 20lb. Luckily he was right: the mirror weighed 21lb 12oz. It was a cracking looking fish and in all probability had never been hooked before.

Before we started fishing the Rother, Neil and I had thought we would be lucky to catch a few fish in the first season and very lucky to catch a twenty, but I had done it with my first fish. It's hard to explain how excited I was with the catch but I did wonder if I had disturbed the swim and if the other fish had moved. I need not have

Dave Passmore with a 24lb 12oz mirror from the River Rother. Note the very big tail and pectoral fins.

worried because, before I could recast, the rod on the far margin was nearly pulled off the buzzer as the Baitrunner went into overdrive. I was convinced that this fish was even bigger, but after a mammoth scrap I netted a common of 12lb or so. It was typical of a lot of the fish I've caught since then, and pound for pound these smaller commons fight harder than any other carp of similar size from a stillwater. It also became clear very quickly that you could guess the size of the fish from the type of fight you got when you hooked them. The bigger fish tended to pick up the bait and power off down the river, but the low double commons charged about all over the river looking for any snag to dive into.

During the remaining hours of darkness I landed another five of these commons and lost three more in a snag that at the time we were unaware of. It later became clear to us that this snag was a hotspot and was the reason there were so many fish in the swim. The prebaiting had merely helped to hold them there. It was also the reason the fish did not leave after each capture. Just as it got light I had another take and again the fish powered off down the river with me in tow, only this time I had the net with me. After much to and froing I finally managed to net the carp in my swim. What a fish. It was a scale-perfect 21lb common. The photograph on page 108 does it justice.

Looking down the river I could see Neil playing a fish so I made my way to him to give help. I arrived just in time to net Neil's first Rother carp. He was pleased with his fish, but when I told him about my night I'm sure that he turned green.

NEIL'S OPENING NIGHT

My swim at the bottom of the straight had some of the features mentioned earlier: forty yards to my right and upstream on the opposite bank was a group of reeds; I put one bait here. Along to my left was a marginal weedbed and the other bait went there. All was quiet through the night, and when I woke in the morning I was surprised that I had had no bleeps at all. I was very disappointed; all the effort in baiting a swim had been for nothing. Because of the other anglers setting up before I arrived, I had no confidence in fishing an area that had not been prebaited and thought that I had no chance of catching. However, at around seven in the morning, as the sun started to warm up, I had the fastest take that I had ever seen.

Sitting on the edge of the bedchair I watched as the tip of the rod whacked round like a good barbel bite before the Baitrunner and the buzzer both went into overdrive simultaneously. Even though I was sitting no more than three feet from the rods, I didn't think that I would be able to pick the rod up before it was pulled from the rests. The take was spectacular but the fight was something else. At this point I will say that I was underpowered in the rod department because I was using a 12ft pound one and three-quarter test curve rods, and they didn't put the fish under enough pressure to control it properly.

The carp charged up and down the river for a distance of forty or fifty yards either side of me. Until it had done virtually what it wanted for ten minutes I could not get it under control. Eventually I was able to net it and I was surprised to find a common of 14lb in the bottom of the net. All through the fight I had wondered what I had hooked because of its power. At one in the afternoon I had a second take from the reeds, and again it fought as though its very life depended on it. Another common was netted, this one weighing 12lb.

The power of these river carp surprised me, but as we caught more fish it was the same story every time with the low double commons. The bigger fish fought completely differently; they took off on long,

Neil Wayte with his first Rother carp, a 14lb 10oz common.

slow powerful runs that had us following them up and down the bank. You couldn't stand your ground and fight them from your swim because they would find the snags every time. More than once I had to follow Dave down the river with the net after he'd hooked a big fish. Even this course of action does not guarantee success every time, as Dave himself will tell you.

During the early part of the season it was possible to fish almost on top of where the fish were holed up, but as the season wore on it became apparent that they would not

tolerate us fishing right on top of them and it became necessary to set up maybe sixty yards away. This produced another problem, however, in that when hooked at sixty yards' range the big fish had the upper hand from the start. We could cope with the smaller commons, but the bigger fish would take line even at this distance and it was necessary to gain line as quickly as possible by running towards the hooked fish and trying to get them on a shorter line. With a lot of line between you and the hook-bait, much of it is laying on the bottom of the river, and this brought another problem: the swan mussels that litter the river bed. On more than one occasion we were cut off before we even picked up the rod, or shortly after picking up the rod. I even played fish with the swan mussels clamped round the line and suspended out of the water.

One night when I was fishing with my wife I had a take at two in the morning and knew straight away that it was a good fish. I followed it down the river, shouting at the wife to get up and bring the net, but when I had gone eighty yards I decided to stand my ground and I clamped down on the spool only for the fish to carry on taking line. This eventually worked and the fish decided to turn back towards my swim. I was happy to let it do this, and on the way back I met Sue coming to see what was wrong. Unfortunately, she didn't have the net with her so she was sent to get it. By the time she returned the line had parted and the fish was gone. On inspecting the line it was chafed and had been damaged by a snag. Up to this point we had caught fish in the low twenties, and I'm convinced that this was bigger than anything we had landed. We will never know. The loss of the fish was disappointing but it encouraged me to carry on. That's the beauty of fishing the Rother: you never know what the next bite will produce.

Back to the opening night, which had started with my confidence very low. By fishing an area that had not previously seen bait, I proved that you could catch fish from anywhere as they moved up and down the river. It also made us wonder how many carp there were in the river because of the number we had caught in the opening twenty-four hours. We were also pleasantly surprised by the size of them. In fact, over the last three years I have only caught one single-figure fish.

Even though it was possible just to drop into a swim and catch, prebaiting is the key to being consistent. My method was to pick a swim in which we had seen fish, and which also gave me several areas to fish to within fifty yards. Each of these features was baited prior to fishing, but Dave came up with a different idea which proved to be more effective both in swims with features on either side of the river, and when fishing new areas or when fishing for just one night.

DIAGONAL LINES

Even though Neil's idea of baiting visible features works, I prefer to bait the river from one side to the other in a diagonal line. I feel that this gives you the chance of picking up fish moving along either margin, as well as any fish moving up the centre of the river. The fish moving along the marginal shelves are more likely to be feeding, whilst the fish travelling up the centre of the river are, to my mind, covering greater distances; a baited area may stop them in their tracks and produce a bonus fish or two. With the diagonal bait pattern, you in effect have three different swims that you could fish from one spot and that are linked by a line of bait.

Now we come to the question of bait. My personal choice for hook-baits and prebaiting is to use boilies because they are easy to use and, like a lot of anglers, I don't get much free time so preparing particles is impractical because I often only decide to fish at the last minute. Boilies are also more selective on the river because if they are of a reasonable size they deter the bream and tench. I caught enough of these when I fished the river previously with corn and hemp. If you like to fish with particles then do so, but I would stick with bigger, harder particles like tigers and maples for hook-baits. Baiting with smaller particles can be very effective, and Richard and Steve Howkins, who have written about the Royal Military Canal, have been successful on the Rother with particles.

Dave Passmore with a 21lb common carp from the Rother.

I do like to use small amounts of trout pellets when I'm fishing, believing that they will pull in smaller fish to the baited area, which helps to attract the patrolling carp. These smaller fish can be a nuisance if you are fishing with softish baits, however, because they will pull a boilie to pieces in a couple of hours. My boilies are made hard if I'm using my homemade baits, but I will often use readymades for convenience. Even these are hard enough to keep on the hair all night without them being pulled to pieces.

One very effective method is to soak your boilies externally rather than put the flavour inside the bait and then boil it, effectively sealing in the flavour. It was whilst testing one of Archie Braddock's flavours that the problem of the small fish came to light, and to combat this I ended up boiling the baits for four minutes to make them hard and then flavouring them prior to freezing. One other way of preparing your bait without boiling out a lot of your flavours is to make the boilies the normal way, with the flavour added to the mix, but instead of placing the finished balls into boiling water you can steam them over boiling water. This skins up the baits to make them hard, but the flavour is not boiled away. It takes a bit of fiddling about with the steaming times to get them right but it's worth the effort.

It's a good tip for winter time, too. Think about it. Most of the fishing on the Rother involves walking to the swims, and when we started fishing the river we carried all our gear on our backs, which meant that by the time we had walked the mile and a half we were totally knackered. When you look at the gear that you carry you will find that a lot of it is not needed, so do yourself a favour and get rid of it. Apart from the tackle, the three heaviest bits of kit are your bedchair, your umbrella and your water. All of these can be exchanged for lighter bits of kit. I replaced my bedchair with an airbed which is extremely comfortable, whilst the big water bottle has been replaced by a small empty bottle and a water filter so that I can get my water from the river. Water filters are quite expensive but you don't have to use them just for the river.

In the summer I use a brolly with storm sides but in winter I used to use a canvas bivvy, which is of course heavy. A trip to a local camping shop produced a replacement for the brolly and bivvy in the shape of a three-man dome. It cost the princely sum of £45 and has yet to let me down. It has the added bonus of having a mosquito door, which on summer nights is a Godsend because the mozzies up the river wear size twelve boots. All rolled up it weighs 8lb and fits inside my rod hod.

Our next step was to purchase a wheelbarrow, which made the trek up the river a lot easier, but it was still hard work pushing it through the long grass. As I found out to my cost, it's easy to break rods when they are strapped on the top. I broke two rods in a week when they snagged in the grass and I couldn't stop in time.

The ultimate piece of kit for river fishing is a boat. Dave's cost nearly £400 but has made transporting fishing tackle up and down the river a pleasure. There is something very relaxing about cruising up the river in a boat, and it also lets you look in areas you would find hard to inspect from the bank. The boat has also come in handy when we have got fish weeded up and have been unable to reach them from the bank.

Well, there you have it, our experiences of carp fishing the Rother. Find your fish and you will catch them. Keep it simple and you won't go far wrong. But most of all, enjoy it. There are miles of river out there with carp swimming in them, and probably not another carp angler for miles.

14 Romney Marsh Drains

By Neil Wayte

The area of Romney Marsh lies to the East of Rye in Sussex and is covered by miles of drains that are used to remove water from the agricultural land. The water level is controlled by the Environment Agency and water is run off the Marsh into the River Rother below the flood control barrier at Scots Float, just outside Rye.

My first visit to the drains came during the summer when I was fishing the Hastings Clubs series of matches. I had become disillusioned with the local carp fishing scene because of the number of people fishing the local waters. Many of them were unemployed, in most cases through no fault of their own, so they were spending a good deal of time on the venues, which made getting a good swim difficult at any time, let alone at weekends.

During the match I noticed a couple of fish bow waving along the far bank of the drain, but try as I might I could not get a bite from them. At the end of the match I asked a couple of the others about them. It appeared that there were quite a few carp in the drain system, but very few people bothered to fish for them. Those that did mainly fished during the winter months because the fish tended to shoal up, which made locating them easier. I made a mental note of this and decided that when the weather got colder I would return to the drain to fish for the carp.

Not being confident enough to tackle the drain alone, I enlisted the help of two friends from work. None of us had fished anything like the drain before so we were completely in the dark as to the whys and wherefores. When I'd fished the drain in the summer there had been plenty of weed cover and marginal reedbeds, which to me were the obvious places to start. In the winter, however, they had died back, leaving only small clumps of weed and patches of dead reed stalks.

These being the only spots that looked likely to hold fish, it was to these that we decided to cast. However, with nearly two miles of drain to choose from, where to actually start was a problem. We decided to fish the drain, as some pike anglers do, by starting at the bottom of the furthest field and leapfrogging our way back to the car park. We spaced ourselves at fifty-yard intervals and fished to any likely looking spot in front of us. After a couple of hours in one swim we would then move above our neighbouring angler and start fishing again. By tackling the venue this way the three of us covered over a mile of bank during the day and it started to give us an idea of how to fish the drain.

If I remember, we only caught one fish that day, a common of 9 or 10lb, and I missed a take. It was enough to whet my appetite. The common that Bob caught was immaculate and it fought like nothing we had ever hooked before, but best of all, particularly for me, was the fact that we were the only three people fishing.

That day saw the start of a four-year obsession with fishing the drain in winter. Sometimes I would do a night shift and then drive straight out to the Marsh to fish all day. It was like having my own fishery, and if I got to the car park and found another car there it would almost spoil the day.

Having said that, it was not the easiest place to fish, which put a lot of people off, and with night fishing not allowed it stopped some from even looking at it. In the winter just getting to the side of the drain was hard work because the first field you had to cross was used by a farmer for growing potatoes. As soon as they were harvested, usually late summer, the field was then ploughed up, which was fine until it rained and then the mud would cling to your boots making walking a real slog. The weather was also a major factor in your fishing. By its very nature there was virtually no cover on the Marsh so the winds would whip across the flat landscape and at times it would feel like it was going to cut you in two. If it was blowing a hooligan it was difficult to walk back to the car with all your tackle without being blown over. Umbrellas didn't last long before being smashed to pieces. Looking back, I was mad to spend as much time as I did out on the Marsh.

As with all types of carp fishing, location is the most important part of the equation, and once located the drain carp were not hard to catch. Truth be known, they were very naive so the fishing was fairly basic. Over a short period of time I developed a style of fishing which proved to be very successful and again allowed me to cover swims quickly and locate the carp.

The drain can be divided into three sections, defined by the field boundaries, with each field being around a mile long. The bottom field was down at water level, and here the drain was some twenty yards wide with a uniform depth of three feet, apart from one short stretch that was a foot deeper. The middle field was raised up and the bank was some fifteen feet above the level of the drain, with sides that were nearly vertical, and width and depth about the same as the bottom field. The last field was not quite as high above the drain, but was still some six feet above the water, although here the drain narrowed to ten yards wide and was shallower, with only eighteen inches to two feet of water.

Along the far bank of the drain were the odd remaining weedbeds or reedbeds, so I would position myself between two of these and cast a bait to each one. Around each I would put twenty freebies, which would be thrown out singly as I was sure that the carp would home in on the splashes and come along to see what was happening. On more than one occasion I had a take before I had put the rod on the buzzer or before I'd put the bobbin on. With the water being so shallow the fish could be spooked very easily, so when setting up I would stay well back from the bank and only approach the drain to put my bank sticks in; even this was done keeping as low as possible, usually crawling on my hands and knees. As I said earlier, I would position myself between two features on the far bank, which could be as much as fifty yards apart, so that I could keep myself away from the areas I was fishing. When I was ready to cast I would walk well back from the edge until I was opposite the weeds or reeds and then creep carefully to the edge and cast out.

Very quickly I found that if there were carp in the area you would get liners almost straight away, so for the first hour I would watch the rod tips for knocks, or the bobbins getting pulled up and down, without takes developing. Initially, I struck these and spooked the fish, but I soon learned that the takes were, how shall I say, 'different' from liners. If after an hour I had no indication at all I would then move on to the next spot. There were times when I would get no indication, then out of the blue I would get a take, but generally I would receive some indication that there were carp present. In the lower field it was not possible to see any indication of the carp feeding, such as water clouding up, because you were so low to the water with the usual breeze! A ripple on the water stopped you from seeing the cloudy water.

However, when fishing in the middle field the higher bank allowed you to walk the length first to see if you could spot cloudy water, or even better spot the carp moving along the far bank. Here again though it paid to keep as low as possible to avoid spooking the fish. Early morning did not prove to be too much of a problem, but as the morning wore on and the sun rose from behind you it would cast a shadow right across the surface of the drain. When this happened I would stay well back from the edge, often with only the last few feet of the drain visible over by the far bank as I walked the length.

If I saw no fish I would again fish to the same features on the far bank and try to get some line bites before moving swims.

The middle field had two different features that were worth fishing to. The most obvious was the two large reedbeds that covered half the width of the drain. These always held fish and a bait fished tight to the base of the reed stems would at some time of the day be picked up. As the light level dropped in the late afternoon, the fish would become more active and it was exciting to sit by your rods watching the reeds move as the carp pushed their way through them, moving closer to your bait. Fishing the reeds required hook and hold tactics, and you couldn't give an inch of line because the reeds cut it like it was cotton. If you positioned yourself either above or below the reeds you could fish one bait towards the far bank and another on the outside of the reedbed in the middle of the drain. This was the only place on the drain that I got a take from the middle; all the others came from no more than three feet from the far bank and I never had a single take from the near margin.

The other feature was the areas of the far bank that had slipped into the water to give a shallow shelf. The carp could often be seen as they crossed over these shallows. Baits placed here were often taken and you could see the fish come up to them. It was also possible to watch them feed and cloud up the water, but I was never lucky enough to see them pick up the hook-bait. Once again, I spent an hour in each area to see if I received any action before moving to another swim.

Tactics for the third field were different because of the depth of the water and the fact that for some reason the weed did not die back as much there. By walking quietly along the bank it was possible to spot groups of fish as they laid up in the weed, and by using light leads and baiting tightly in holes in the weed it was possible to catch them. I didn't spend as much time fishing the third field because the carp did not spend much time there; however, there were occasions when, for whatever reason, large numbers of carp would be present.

Winter was the best time to fish the drain because the carp tended to shoal up and multiple catches were possible. It was possible to catch from the drain in all types of weather conditions. Even in freezing-cold easterly winds you could get a take or two, providing you knew where to fish. During one such freezing cold easterly wind I was fishing down on the lower field without any success and had decided to call it a day, but instead of walking across the field back to the car I decided to follow the path of the drain to see if I could spot any fish. As I walked along the high banks of the middle field I noticed two fish laying up under the far bank, and just a few yards further on I spotted somewhere in the region of 300 carp all lying side by side within a yard of the far bank. The shoal must have stretched for thirty yards; I think that the majority of the drain's carp were in this area which was sheltered from the effects of the wind.

I spent all afternoon trying to catch them but they were just not interested in feeding. I even tried fishing a pop-up straight up

Neil Wayte with a typical common, of 14lb 10oz, from White Kemp on the Romney Marshes.

from the lead on an 18in hook length so that the bait was sitting right in amongst them, but it was still ignored.

Although I failed on that day the swim went on to produce many fish for me, including my second 20lb common. The best time to fish the drain was without doubt when a big south-westerly was blowing; it made fishing difficult but the carp loved it and went on the feed. On one February afternoon I caught eight carp before I ran out of bait and the shoal moved down the drain towards another angler. Interestingly, the carp got bigger and bigger. The first one was around 8lb, and by the last fish they were up to 14lb. The angler below me had a further four fish which started off at

14lb and reached 18lb by the last fish. On that afternoon I went through a six-egg mix of 14mm baits, which is a lot of bait to use in the middle of winter and still run out! After that day I always took a lot of bait with me just in case.

The second exceptional day didn't see me land many fish; I did manage nine takes but I only landed three, all commons of 9lb. I lost the biggest fish I had seen at the net, a common of maybe 25lb. Try as I might, I could not get them to stay on. I went from light leads to heavy ones, from size eight hooks to size twos, from supple hook links to stiff links, but nothing seemed to make much difference. Each time I got a take I just wondered how long it would stay on before the hook pulled. Very frustrating.

The strangest thing to happen during my time on the drain occurred one foggy February morning. I arrived just before it got light and was setting up in the bottom field when I heard a slurping noise coming from the far bank. Most of you will know the sound that a carp makes when taking baits from the surface. At first I thought I was hearing things, but before it became light I heard it three or four times. Surely the carp weren't feeding on the surface in February?

When it finally got light I saw a pair of lips break the surface close to the far bank. I rummaged through the bottom of my rucksack and found a small bag of mixers. More out of hope than anything else I fired a few out and let them drift down on the current to where the fish was taking. As they passed over the fish it rose and took a couple. I fired out four small pouches of mixers at varying distances upstream, and then quickly set up the third rod with a small controller. By casting opposite myself and keeping the line out of the water by holding the rod in the air it was easy to let the controller run down the far margin towards the fish. Three times I let it pass right over the spot were the fish had been taking without getting a take, so on the fourth run through I put the rod down on the reeds and rolled a cigarette. Although I wasn't holding the rod I kept an eye on where the mixer was, and it suddenly dawned on me that the controller was coming towards me against the current!

I quickly recovered the slack line and struck into a very solid fish that just did not want to come up off the bottom. This continued for four or five minutes without me making any impression, until the fish evidently decided that it had had enough, turned and began to swim powerfully away from me. I picked up the net and began to follow it down the drain when suddenly the hook pulled. By the way it had fought staying on the bottom of the drain it was obviously one of the better fish, but I will never

know how big. It would have made a good story, catching it off the top in February, but it was not to be.

Having said earlier that it pays to be quiet and keep low when setting up and fishing, I sometimes did the complete opposite to try to locate the carp. This trick was only relevant to the bottom field but would often lead to a bonus fish or two. If I was fishing in the middle of the bottom field and things were slow, I would wait until the sun had risen behind me, then walk back into the field and make my way to the bottom before I approached the edge. My shadow would then fall across the surface of the drain, and slowly I would walk back towards where I was fishing. As my shadow moved along the far margin it would spook any fish that were lying up there. They always spooked away from the shadow and towards my swim. When I got within fifty yards of the swim I would then walk away from the edge so that my shadow was no longer on the water and would creep back to my rods. The disturbed fish would never go much further than fifty yards or so and it had the effect of herding them like sheep towards my swim.

Throughout the four winters I spent fishing on the drain I landed nearly 180 fish; only three of those were mirrors, and the majority of the commons ranged from high singles to low doubles, but what they lacked in size they made up for with the fight they gave. You soon learnt the difference between line bites and takes. Virtually every take resulted in the tip of the rod whacking round and the Baitrunner exploding into life. Even if you sat right on the rods you were always worried that you'd never pick the rod up before it was dragged from the rests with the violence of the take. When fishing to the large reedbeds the Baitrunner was turned off so that the fish could not dive straight into the beds, but you had to be alert all the time and watch for the slightest indication so you were ready for the take when it came.

Fishing the drain was probably the most exciting fishing I had done because you never knew what was coming next. A friend even had a 20lb-plus pike on a pop-up. I only stopped fishing the drain when I thought I had taken it as far as I could. I landed two 20lb commons and a mirror of 19lb 14oz, and apart from the big common I lost at the net I never saw anything enormous. However, having said that, there are miles of drains on the Marsh that receive very little angling pressure so there could well be some big fish out there. All of the drains are connected, with very few obstructions, so they could turn up anywhere at any time!

15 The River Severn

Mark Law

The River Severn is one of the largest rivers in England, but despite holding numbers of carp it is not heavily fished. For the size of the river it does not receive any sort of pressure at all; only a few groups of anglers tackle the river, and even fewer individuals spend time fishing the river for carp. I know only of Ian Poole and his mate Mick Howells from the Tewkesbury area, who, along with a couple of other anglers, have put in time on the river.

The Severn is a bit of an unknown quantity, and for this reason carp anglers today seem to give it a miss. If it were seen in the angling press that a mass of thirties and forties were taken there every week, then the Severn – and any other river for that matter – would be the 'in' place to fish. But when little or nothing is written or published, no one tends to fish the rivers. The simple fact is that nobody wants to be a pioneer these days.

With so many people carp fishing it is no wonder that when somebody does catch something special, or starts to catch quite a few carp, they want to keep quiet about it. This was the case with myself – until now.

My association with the Severn started in 1997. I had been working for Foster's of Birmingham, and before that Gold Label Tackle and Birmingham Angling Centre, but after leaving the tackle trade I felt that a new challenge was needed – hence the Severn. But where to start?

The only way to make sure that you are in the right spot is to see your quarry, and this can only be done on a river the size of the Severn with absolutely loads of leg work.

You must get off your backside and go for it because the fish will not come to you. Just because you see fish on a river, it does not mean they feed in that particular spot, but it does give you somewhere to start. Finding the fish has got to be your number one priority; sounds easy, but with miles and miles of bank, on both sides of the river remember, it is the hardest thing about river carping.

Several people had mentioned a particular area to me over the years, so this had to be the first place to look. I breed and show dogs, so the first time I walked the section was on the way back from a show. I walked about half a mile upstream and the same downstream and saw nothing. I was with my wife and kids so it turned out to be a nice walk along the river bank. The dogs had a nice stroll too, but after a two-mile hike it became apparent that this was something I would have to do alone.

Two weeks later, on the hottest day so far that summer, I was on my sixth trip, still just looking, when I saw my first River Severn carp – a nice double of about 16lb. The more I looked the more I found. I saw a group of twelve carp, mainly singles, with a couple of doubles thrown in for good measure. Four pegs along I found a couple of better fish: two twenties were looking straight at me, like two submarines waiting for the enemy. It soon became apparent that I had found a feeding area, because a few of the fish were coming in to the marginal shelf bubbling, fizzing and colouring up the water.

I was lucky to find this feeding spot, but generally I believe in making your own luck;

by spending so much time just being there I had made my own luck. Once I'd found what I was looking for I started to walk back to the car. It had been around four hours since I spotted the first fish, but only twenty yards away from the feeding spot and around the same distance out in the river I spotted two more fish. They were swimming towards me so I pulled my Optics down over my eyes to get a better view. I had to look twice because in front of me were two fish that were possibly in the 40lb bracket. The excitement was fantastic. I knew the river record was an incredible 39lb 7oz but I never thought I would see a fish of this size, let alone two. This was turning out to be a good day: I had found the fish, I had found an area holding fish, and I'd found a feeding spot. This was one thing … the bait, tackle and baiting up tactics were going to be something else.

As you can imagine, I spent the drive home working out a game plan. The first thing I had to know was what the bottom of the river was like, so I decided to take my nine-foot inflatable boat and echo sounder for a proper look around. One hour with the echo sounder is worth a day with a marker float. The bottom was fairly uniform, with a marginal shelf which was three feet deep, dropping to four and a half feet further out. The river bed steadily dropped off to the centre of the river, a depth of twelve feet. It was the four-and-a-half-foot shelf that took my fancy, but I planned to try different depths in order to find the optimum feeding spots – if such things existed of course. I realize that not everyone has the option of using an inflatable boat and echo sounder, but you only have to use such items once.

I must also stress that when using a boat you must always wear a life jacket. Good quality jackets are available that do not cost the earth. Never go out in a boat without one. I must also mention here that the boat was only used for feature finding and not fish finding.

With all of the technical side sorted out it was time to think about bait. There were many options open to me. Should I use a particle? If so, which one? Should I use a combination of particles? The list of particle baits available is mind blowing to someone coming into carp fishing, so I will list the most popular ones: tiger nuts, hempseed, buckwheat, Hinders Partiblend and peanuts are all favourites of mine. Other items which I use as a second line of attack include maple peas, chickpeas and groats.

Half of me wanted to go in with the particle approach but the other half of me didn't. I had better explain my thinking here. Firstly, the reasons for using particles are that they are cheap (unless you use tiger nuts), or should I say that they are economical, easy to prepare and readily available. The carp go for them in a big way, which is all good stuff. However, using particles on a river does have its downside. You must take into account the flow, which may be different from the last time that you fished. To combat the flow I have found that using groundbait mixed into large balls with as much particle in there as possible helps to get the particles to the bottom of the river. Some of these balls may weigh as much as two pounds (these were put in to position using the boat).

I have found that the more accurately you bait, the better the fishing, so with this in mind I decided against using the particles to save me having to take the boat every time. Most of my fishing would be done on overnighters so taking the boat was just not feasible. With the decision made not to use particles the obvious choice was the good old boilie. Now there's a bait: bird food, protein and fishmeal to name but a few, and the same problem as with the particles – which one to use? I never, and I mean never, use protein baits, and with the amount of baiting-up I would have to do it would have been too expensive anyway. I'm not a great believer in the protein bait theory, but if people want to use that sort of thing then as with all aspects of carp fishing you must use what you feel comfortable with. Give me a good old fishmeal or bird food any day of the week.

I was to be fishing in the height of summer and wanted a base mix which would be similar to the food the carp were used to, so I chose the fishmeal option. The mix I used was one of my own which I have used for a number of years on many different waters:

4oz Full fat soya flour
1oz Ground rice
2oz CLO bird food
2oz Nectarblend
8oz White fishmeal

This base mix has served me well over the years and can be adjusted to include more fishmeal or more bird food. I forgot to mention earlier that I like to use birdfood ingredients in my fishmeal base mixes as I feel that these help to disperse the flavour at a better rate. You also get the best of both worlds because you are giving the carp a choice: if they like bird food they will eat it; if they like fishmeal they will eat it; if they like both then all the better. What I'm trying to get over is the fact that with the two ingredients in there you can get the carp feeding on the bait better, and up to the time of writing I have caught carp over 20lb from twenty-seven different venues so I feel I'm more than qualified in terms of catching carp.

Again, as soon as we sorted out one problem another one arose – flavours. More decisions. I could write all day on this subject, but if there is one flavour I would use above all others it would have to be John Baker's Limited Edition Plum. Many, many carp have graced my landing net with the help of this particular flavour. Instant, that's what I call it. So the choice of flavour was the easiest of all my decisions. I use it at the

rate of 3.5ml per six-egg mix. It is better to use it at this level if you are going to bait up heavily; any more and the bait could have a short life span. Once I started to catch on a regular basis I would drop the flavour by half a mil. By doing this I could keep the bait working, and if it started to die I would drop the flavour by another half a mil. The Plum was the only additive in the base mix because I felt that these fish had not seen anything boilie-wise so I would just keep it simple and offer them something they were going to want to eat and eat. If the chub and barbel didn't get there first, of course.

If the bait were to start to die a little and dropping the flavour level didn't help, then I would add one and a half mil of Solar's Esterblend 12 and bring the Plum down to two and a half mil. You must have a game plan, so to speak. This was to be an all or nothing attempt at catching a very large river carp so everything had to be just right. Nothing could be left to chance; if you hit a problem the answer had to be to hand.

As for quantity – where would you start? There was only one way to go as far as I was concerned and that was heavy. The nuisance fish had to be overcome and the carp had to accept the bait as a natural food source, so it just had to be heavy. I gave myself a start date (remember there is a close season on the rivers) which was the second week of the season. This, I felt, would get the opening week madness out of the way.

I decided to bait up with ten kilos of bait per visit, and this presented me with another problem – making all that bait. Ten kilos sounds like a lot of bait, but it doesn't take long to throw it in the river! I borrowed a compressor and air bait gun from a friend so the rolling was made easier. Rolling? Who said anything about rolling? I saved myself loads of time by using a Solar four nozzle adapter along with a Gardner 18mm roller. By putting a twelve-egg mix into the gun and running it across the bait table

Mark Law with the River Severn record: a carp of 42lb 2oz.

twice I had eight sausages, and then I just pushed the top of the roller down on to them, creating little pillows. It was much quicker like this and had the advantage that once the pillows were in the river they wouldn't roll along the river bed. The bait does not go as far in the catapult, but because I was baiting up with a Cobra baiting spoon or by hand it didn't cause a problem.

I think I have covered everything now apart from tackle, and I will discuss that later in the chapter.

The time had arrived for me to bait up, so bait up I did. During the first week I visited the river on three occasions – Monday, Wednesday and Friday – and the following week I started on Sunday, visiting again on Tuesday and Thursday. This was the pattern that I wanted to keep to. I made a point of not visiting the river on a Saturday night

because it would be busy with barbel anglers and I did not want to have to explain myself to anyone at midnight, or at any other hour for that matter. The first five visits just saw me going down to bait up. I would get to the swims about half an hour before dark and I would always take one of my Japanese Akita dogs with me, the reasons being that they are good company, and because the only other people I saw were usually dog walkers so it made sense to try to blend in. It gave me an ideal excuse for being there because you never know who you are going to bump into.

After five nights of baiting up over a ten-day period I was ready to do my first night's fishing on the Severn for carp. As usual I arrived at the swim just before dark and the anticipation and expectations were high. One carp, that's all I wanted, just one. I tried to keep the tackle to a minimum

119

because I wanted to get to and from the car as quickly as possible. Carp tackle sticks out like a sore thumb. I fished with two baits in four and a half feet of water to my right, and the other two slightly further out in six feet of water to my left. Because my baiting had been done just before dark I introduced two kilos of bait when I started and planned to top up the swim if nuisance fish became a problem. The remainder of the bait would be put in as I left in the morning.

The first night was a bit of an anti-climax as no carp slipped up, but a couple of chub in the 3lb bracket were caught, both on the close in rods. I packed up at 5am after staying awake all night to see if anything showed itself, but unfortunately nothing did.

The following week saw me fish for two nights and bait up on the third. I caught two more chub whilst fishing, but on the third night, as I was spooning out the boilies, two carp showed in the swims. The first rolled on the surface but the second jumped clear of the water. You can imagine my excitement at seeing these fish as I stood in the swim; unfortunately, my tackle was at home. It did cross my mind to rush home to get it but we had a dog show the following day so the carp would have to wait.

I couldn't wait until the next time I was able to go fishing. Back in the swim two days later I was really expecting it to happen, and at 1.30am it did. The only trouble was that it was another chub, quickly followed by two more. All of these were caught on the close in rods so I decided to move the two other rods closer in, on to the four-and-a-half-foot shelf. A couple of quick casts and a kilo of bait later and I was laying back on the bedchair when a full blooded run developed on the far right-hand rod. I was on it in a flash – well, after I had picked myself up after falling off the bedchair. Here I was in the dark playing a fish and I knew exactly what it was on the other end. After two good runs the fish decided to play ball and into the net it went. Yes! I looked at my prize, a mirror of 17lb 8oz, took a couple of quick photos and was just about to recast as the right-hand rod burst into life. Another angry carp headed for the middle of the river, but with 15lb Big Game and 25lb Kryston Merlin I had other ideas. It was soon apparent that this one was a bit smaller. It was in the net quickly and released none the worse for its ordeal. I don't think either carp had been caught before and things were looking good with a seventeen- and fifteen-pounder in one night. But it didn't stop there because before dawn three more doubles had graced my net.

As Hannibal used to say on the Team – I love it when a plan comes together! All the hard work had started to pay off, finally. It was a good feeling that morning on the drive home. It was now time to ease off on the baiting, so on each visit I was going to use half of what I had started with. My next visit should have been just to bait up, but because of my little result I was going to fish. Strike whilst the iron's hot, as they say.

Back in the swim less than two days later and conditions were the same, south-westerly wind, nice and warm, and dark with no moon. The carp were in the swim, that's for sure. At roughly 1am a large carp jumped clean out of the water at a distance of two rod lengths out, right over the left-hand rod. Over the space of an hour the carp jumped another four times and I kept thinking – any moment now. Despite all the excitement I must have dozed off to sleep because at 3.45am I had a screamer on the left-hand rod. This fish was taking line at an alarming rate as it moved off to the left. This was the one place that I didn't want the carp to go because there were a couple of overhanging trees in the water that I knew had branches going into the river; I had checked them out earlier in the summer. By now the fish had made the snags, much to my annoyance, so I opened the bail arm and let the fish keep running with no pressure on the line whatsoever. I let it have ten yards or

A stunning sunset over the River Severn.

so and then I hit it hard. The rod was kept low and I just pulled as hard as I could. Remarkably, the beast just did not know what had hit it and I managed to pump it all the way to the net. My first thoughts were: 'a monster!'. No monster but at 23lb 14oz I was not complaining. My decision to fish had been the right one.

Everything was going to plan so I just had to keep on going and maybe, just maybe, I would hook one of the chunks. The next two sessions were blanks, followed by a couple of nights of doubles. As time went by it became easier to read the river and the best conditions were on the darkest nights with a south-westerly wind. By now I had stopped the baiting-up apart from when I was actually fishing, which was two nights a week. It was now September and the fishing was about the same; I would catch a couple

of doubles and then have a couple of blanks. The largest carp was still the twenty-three-pounder.

On a cool, rather windy night in September I was back in the swim. It had rained the week before and as a result the fishing had suffered. I had blanked on both visits. Nothing happened through the night, but as I was about to pack up the left-hand rod tore off at an alarming rate of knots. Before I knew it the carp was nearly straight across the river, and then for good measure it decided it would be a good idea to kite left. This was the worst thing possible because to the left were the snags. When you have a big fish on a long line and it's kiting some-where you don't want it to, I find the best thing is to try to pull the same way as the fish is travelling. This was the only option left to me. I started to pile on the pressure and it worked well, as the fish didn't know what had hit it.

Soon there were big boils coming up and then a great big carp rolled on the surface. A further minute later and she was in the net. My first impression was that I'd caught a thirty, but on the scales she went: 29lb 14oz. An exceptional river carp but not one of the two chunks I had seen earlier in the season. I put the remaining bait in and decided to come back that evening.

At this time I was having trouble with 4oz dumpy leads moving in the flow, so I started to make my own 5oz flat dumpies. At the time I didn't realize just what effect this would have on me, because when I met up with my old mate Roy Russell we got chatting and it became apparent that he also made his own leads. We put two and two together and came up with our own company – Camo Leads. We like to think that we have a coating for all situations, so there is something for everyone.

Back to the fishing. I returned that evening, and there was a definite buzz in the air, especially after the big mirror of the night before. Everything was set in exactly the same way as it had been every other night that I had fished on the river. Conditions were the same as the previous night. It looked good for another fish but nothing happened until 2.30am when a barbel of about 6lb decided to go on a mad rampage around the right of the swim. It must have taken five minutes to subdue it and get it into the large landing net. I was glad that it had all happened on the right of the swim because it was on the left that all of my previous action had taken place.

All of a sudden the left-hand rod came to life. At first I thought it was a chub because of the nature of the take, but as I picked up the rod I knew straight away that this was no chub. As with the two previous large carp this one moved off to the left, not with speed but with brute force. I managed to get the side strain on quickly and pulled as hard as I dared, successfully bringing the leviathan in front of me where it proceeded to go on three more powerful runs. Each time it headed towards the snags as it obviously knew they were there. I must have played it for fifteen minutes before it came anywhere near the margin. It broke the surface and it was obviously a very big carp. My heart was in my mouth as it went round the margin, then it was all over as I managed to guide it over the drawstring and into the net. Yeeeees!

Up on to the scales via the landing net pole. The more I lifted, the more the dial kept going until it settled at 42lb 2oz – a new English personal best and a River Severn record. I sacked the beast whilst I decided what to do. Did I risk the self-photography or did I go and get Sharon to come and do the honours? I decided on the latter. The fish was sacked up in a safe place; I made sure it was in good shape otherwise I wouldn't have left it. The journey home was made in double quick time. Sharon wondered what the hell was happening when I woke her at 4.15am, but fifteen minutes later she and the kids were ready and we all went off towards the river. We got back and the fish was none the worse for its ordeal. With the photographs done it was time to release her back to her own environment. She swam off strongly. It may sound strange but I felt very sorry that I had put this fantastic creature through such an ordeal.

That was the last time I fished the river. There was no need to go back as I had done what I wanted to, and as you can see from the photographs it's a wonderful fish. I hope you enjoyed reading this piece as much as I enjoyed writing it. See you next time.

16 The River Soar

Terry Brookes

Although a tributary of the River Trent, the River Soar, which flows through Leicestershire, taking in small parts of Nottinghamshire and Warwickshire, has a great history of its own. Boats have used the Soar since pre-Roman days, but contrary to my friend and angling author Paul Dennis's stories, I do not remember them!

In the eighteenth century, the river was improved in stages for navigation, part of the amazing nationwide network of waterways built at the time. Boats could then easily transport goods and materials needed by people and industry; the rivers were the motorways of their day. Today the River Soar is used for relaxation rather than for industry, but you can still travel by boat northwards to the Rivers Trent and Humber, and southwards to London. The main tributaries of the Soar are the Rivers Wreake, Sence and the Rothley Brook.

The Grand Union Canal also joins, leaves and rejoins the river at various points along its flow, from its narrow start at Burbage to the point at which it joins the River Trent at Ratcliffe on Soar. The river is often underrated by carp anglers but, believe me, the carp are there. My biggest landed fish to date is 25lb 3oz taken on hair-rigged sweetcorn; however, there is proof that fish over 30lb are also in the river.

The River Soar and its catchment is an area of high archaeological potential, with evidence of human occupation in this part of middle England over the last 500,000 years. The present course of the river follows the route of a major prehistoric river, the 'Midlands River', which flowed from the Midlands across East Anglia and into the North Sea basin. This course is believed to have been the route followed by some of the early colonists of Britain, and their tools have been found at various locations along the river's route.

The Soar has been a major resource of food, transport and power, and has been the location of major settlements, such as Leicester, during the Iron Age, Roman, Medieval and post-Medieval periods. Buried beneath the alluvium of the river and its tributaries are the tools, settlements, water-mills and bridges which indicate human occupation in the area.

Below Leicester the river is in its senile stage, and can be seen as an example of better known old rivers, such as the American lower Mississippi. North of Leicester the river meanders through a broad and beautiful flood plain. On either side, the old villages of Wanlip, Birstall and Thurmaston look out over a lowland landscape of rivers, meadows, lakes and woodlands.

Perhaps one of the most famous bridges in English history crossed the River Soar. Bow Bridge, in Leicester itself, was the setting for the beginning of the Tudor reign. In 1484, Richard III rode out of Leicester over the river, over Bow Bridge, on his way to do battle with Henry Tudor at Bosworth Field. Going over the bridge, his foot hit one of the stones that made up the bridge. He rode out a crowned king. He came back a naked corpse, slung over his horse, whereupon his head banged against the same stone! His remains were thrown off the bridge and into the River Soar. And so began the strong rule

Terry with a heavily scaled Soar carp.

of the Tudor monarchs.

This is just a little of the River Soar's colourful past. The river is full of history, and more importantly it's full of fish. As for the future, I am confident that anglers will continue to catch big fish from a river I would describe as flowing through some of England's most pleasant countryside.

Carp – that magical word that sets your heart racing. And the fish of Leicestershire's River Soar are no exception. Believe it or not, until the closure of the enormous power station in Raw Dykes Road in Leicester itself, the mile straight was one of the best carp waters in the country. Nowadays, however, anglers can find the lumps they crave along most of the river's length, from Watermead Way, north of Leicester city, right up to the point at which it joins the River Trent. The canalized sections of the river also contain a good head of carp, especially near the factories, where the workers feed them every day. But with most anglers preferring solitude, I will look at the areas that could give you the best results. And it's worth remembering that a good recce is always worthwhile, as is knowing who controls the fishing rights, and whether night fishing is allowed or not.

From Watermead Way the river runs north through the Watermead Country Park. Parts of this stretch are canalized and are surrounded by some beautiful lakes and countryside. Some of the lakes also contain carp, and are worth a look. Maps are available for this area – north, central and south of Leicester – which give a good plan of the waterway. These maps, 'Leicester's Riverside Park', can be obtained free from riverside rangers and project development officers (tel: 0116 252 7297). These will take you as far as the Wanlip area, and are well worth looking at for the information they contain.

Mirrors like this are plentiful on the Soar.

With that area covered, we can now start at Rothley. This is situated on the A6, Leicester to Loughborough road, and again has a very interesting past. Going into Rothley from Leicester on the old road, turn right at the traffic lights, there's a nice old pub on the corner that provides a really good service, and the river is just a short way down the road.

We are talking carp waters here, although it must be said that it is rare to find the specimen anglers taking advantage of the river's potential in this area. Both sides of the road bridge going over the river are worth trying, but to your right the river splits and goes into the Grand Union Canal. To the right of the fork, the river has no boat traffic except the odd canoe. This part of the river contains some very big carp. It has been a holding area for big fish for many, many years, with fish reaching the high twenties. One of the favoured and most productive

methods here is to lay down a good bed of hemp close in, and to fish corn, meat, lobworm or boilie over it. Floating baits and stalking can also be productive, whilst baits like crust, marshmallows and dog biscuits are regular catchers. The odd big fish has been landed at the back end of the year but summer months are considered best.

To the left of the road bridge, heading towards Sileby, the river meets all the requirements needed for river carp. The same methods are used, and again this section is untapped by the specialists. It is always worth walking the section before setting up.

Towards the island, carp can be seen just roving about and are well worth stalking. As with most river carp anglers, I find an expedition during May most helpful. You can find the areas that look likely to produce, and if, like me, you live close by, a little prebaiting on a regular basis in your fancied swims can be useful. It also gives you the chance to suss out any relevant information from fellow anglers.

Heading towards Sileby, the closer to the marina the more carp you are likely to find; the boat owners keep them more or less as pets! But there are also very good swims away from the marina that produce fish into the mid-twenties. In this area there are facilities that include camp sites, shops and all the things that make a trip enjoyable, like a good watering hole!

From Sileby onwards to the River Trent, the carp fishing improves by Barrow upon Soar. If you are looking to spend a holiday fishing for River Soar carp, then Barrow upon Soar has the lot. There is a big camp site, called Proctors Pleasure Park, from where you can camp and fish, or camp and travel the area (tel: 01509 412434). The shopping facilities are excellent, and the next village, Mountsorrell, has a very good tackle shop called Bennetts (tel: 0116 230 2818). As a bonus, the female boss, Leslie, is a first-class carp angler and will put you right on all local matters, such as tickets, baits and so on.

My own personal best river carp came out at Barrow upon Soar. There are so many different opportunities for catching, and it's up to the individual angler to pick his or her own method. There is very deep slow water, fast water, deep weir pools, reedbeds and lily pads. The best advice I can give about the (roughly) three-mile stretch from Barrow upon Soar to Cotes Mill is to have a day out exploring the river. Walk the bank, talk to the regular anglers – they don't bite! It would be wrong for me to suggest certain swims and methods, as we carp anglers do tend to do things our own way and keep swims a closely guarded secret. Without doubt though, the best area is the 'Old Soar' route, the backwater.

A typical Soar mirror for Terry.

This part of the river comes down over the weir at Pillings Lock and goes for miles uninterrupted by boat traffic. This is a season ticket water, and is possibly one of the best tickets to be in possession of. It is full of big fish of many species. Loughborough Soar AC is the controlling body, and a good contact is Rod Hubbard at Soar Valley Tackle (tel: 01509 231817). This stretch is known to hold carp over the 30lb mark.

As previously stated, I am not one to advise other anglers on methods to use, but I do believe in the old advice given to soldiers: K.I.S.S. or Keep It Simple Stupid! There is no real need for fancy rigs on the Soar. My own regular method is a straight Korda lead, hair rig and bait when sitting and waiting. My rods are Daiwa Powermesh 2.5lb test curve twinned with Shimano Baitrunners filled with Ashima line and Ashima hooks. Having declared there's no need for fancy rigs, I suppose there are times when a different approach can be used in certain swims. But generally speaking, keep it simple.

As for baits, well, again it's a matter of personal choice. Boilies, sweetcorn, luncheon meat, sausage, Peperami, you name it and carp have been caught on it. There is, however, a leaning towards hair rigged meat at present, either natural or flavoured.

It is not uncommon when fishing tight in to use a good flavoured paste. I tend to go for the Marukya range of baits, including the giant casters and the giant flavoured corn, but that's a personally proven choice. There are no hard and fast rules for fishing this part of the river, but it's only fair to advise you that, having set out my stall one day for carp on meat, my day ended with chub to 6lb, barbel to 8lb and a couple of decent pike! But that's the way it goes sometimes. And in reverse, I have fished the waggler for roach and bream, only to be left

Terry with a scatter-scaled mirror.

Fishing amongst the reeds.

rubbing what's left of my hair after latching on to a few lumps.

Access to this stretch of pristine river is by good old-fashioned walking. There are points at which to leave vehicles depending upon which stretch you will be fishing, but at some point you are going to be walking and carrying your gear. Some anglers look like they are in training for the SAS when they cross the fields. So have a recce before you decide your pegs.

One area at Barrow upon Soar that is also worth a mention is the are around The Navigation public house. During the writing of this chapter, a footbridge has been erected over the weir behind the pub. This certain-ly reduces the walking time to some of the very good swims between Barrow upon Soar and Sileby, when approaching the river from the Barrow end. There are also some houses on the opposite side to the tow path whose gardens back down to the water's edge, so anglers should be careful regarding their habits when fishing!

It's well worth carp-watching along this particular stretch. The choice of waters to fish in this area is great. It is a fact that carp over 20lb are being caught regularly, and weighed. There are carp in the first weir that you cross, and also in the backwaters that circle the area. The weir crossed by the new bridge is mainly a big chub water, but on the slower water carp can be caught, although it is a very slow catching area.

The baits for use on this stretch can vary from day to day. During the warmer weather, fruit-flavoured boilies can be productive, and meat and corn also work well. I usually have two different hook-baits out at the same time when fishing right over the river. Fishing close in is a different kettle of fish, so to speak. A good bed of hemp against the pads is an attractor, with meat, corn, lobworm and even bread over the top. Summertime produces a lot of boat traffic in this area, so a line close in is always advisable; I have taken carp to 20lb on this method.

There is an excellent head of carp all along this area. When you do hit the right swim along this stretch you can expect more than just the one fish during the session; it's not unknown for anglers to land up to eight fish on a good day. That is a fair day out in my opinion – you are talking 100lb of carp!

In the Cotes Mill area of the river are one or two swims that produce good carp catches. Close to the Mill itself is a good catching area. There have been a lot of improvements to the banks in this area, but the fishing has not been disturbed.

Going out towards Cotes from Loughborough on the B676, you will come to Cotes Mill. A bank walk is advisable here. If you walk upriver, back towards Barrow upon Soar, the choice of swims is enormous. You can really get settled in and do some comfortable fishing. The pegs are on the opposite side to Cotes Mill. Downstream, the river twists and turns, and there are a few shallow runs, so stalking is recommended. Carp are active all the way up to Normanton on Soar.

The Hathern area contains carp upwards from 20lb and is worth looking at. Just follow the A6 out of Loughborough, from which you can see the river. There are various public houses along the route, and a quick pint and chat could get you all the up-to-date local information required for a

good session. The natives are friendly in this area.

Continuing along the A6 towards junction 24 of the M1, Kegworth has produced good carp catches over the years, and continues to produce some really big fish. We are now coming towards the end of the River Soar, to the point at which it joins the River Trent. A close study of local maps will show you where various locks are situated, as well as any obstructions that may hinder you.

Red Hill Lock has drastically changed over the years, but the carp are still there. Summertime can be an ordeal though, due to the boat traffic. Access to this area is fairly easy, and a stroll will help you find the features you require for a good day out. The locals around the marina are worth approaching as they tend to see the fish moving about.

That just about concludes my quick guide to the River Soar and its carp. Where to catch the lumps? Well, the choice is now yours. No doubt some people will argue about the river and its contents, the baits to use, and most other things that have been written over the years. I can only state the facts as I know them from my own experiences. There are carp over the 30lb mark in the Soar, that's a fact. It is not a magical carp-catching water, though; you do have to work at it. The river has been ignored in the past, except by those in the know, and photographs have rarely appeared in the angling press of those fish caught.

Myself, I have enjoyed fishing the river for carp for many years, and I hope to continue for many years to come. I am not an angling author, just an ordinary chap who enjoys his sport, and hopefully I have recorded an honest opinion to help other anglers understand what the River Soar is all about. I do foresee that in the future more will be heard of the Soar and its carp. All I can hope is that you enjoy your visit to the river, walk the banks, talk to people, and may you all have good sport with lots of the River Soar's lumps.

USEFUL CONTACTS:

Awsworth and Cossall AC	0115 932 4255
Broome AC	0116 235 7210
Cobden AC	0115 973 3253
Jelson AC	0116 266 6911
Kegworth AC	0115 928 5390
Leicester and District	0116 266 6911
Long Eaton and District	0115 972 7164
Long Eaton Victoria	0115 972 4813
Loughborough Soar AC	0150 921 0927
Nottingham AA	0115 978 2630
Quorn AC	0150 941 3442
Shaftsbury AC	0115 973 2910
Slack and Parr AC	0150 967 3536
Sutton Bonington Anglers	0150 967 4873
Zingari AC	01332 872170

17 The River Thames

Andy Dixon

I have fished the Thames around my area for a good many years, but for most of those years have caught only smaller inhabitants, taking quivertip rods down to Kingston and catching the shy old bream, or fishing tight into the margins with a worm in the winter for wide-shouldered roach that hid from the powerful currents.

Trotting a small hair quilled float along next to various boats for the shoals of dace that flashed in and out of houseboat anchor chains was another distraction, and the audacious perch also felt my hook; a large lobworm chucked into the frothing waters of Teddington Weir produced a stunning fish of just under 4lb.

On the odd occasions an unseen monster has captured my imagination. One such encounter occurred when I was fishing for bream along the Canberry Gardens stretch of the Thames at Kingston. It was early winter and I was fishing with a friend. We were both casting out towards a concrete man-made island with swimfeeders loaded with maggots and groundbait, and watching for the slightest movement on the tips of our rods. There was a vast amount of rubbish floating down the river, ranging from small twigs to huge branches; these we tried to avoid where possible.

We had both had our fair share of fish when I hit yet another typical bream bite. The fish slowly moved downstream. It was very heavy and after a short while I thought I had lost it and had simply become entangled with one of the branches floating past us. Then, the branch changed direction and headed upstream. This was very odd, and

as I was blissfully unaware that branches could swim, especially against a strong winter current, the thought slowly came to me that maybe this 'branch' could be something other than a section of decapitated tree.

Whatever it was had now made its way speedily upstream, with me just holding on and watching the line get lower and lower on the spool of my reel. Eventually I grabbed the reel tightly in my hand and refused to give any more line, hoping to turn whatever it was. Unfortunately, the inevitable happened and the line sang in the wind for a few seconds, the rod bent into a back-wrenching curve, and all went slack. The line had parted and I was left wondering what on earth had been on the end of it.

On another occasion I was fishing for dace on a stretch of river further upstream, near Surbiton, at a very small section called the Slipway. During the morning I had caught many dace and the odd roach, with a very unusual trout thrown in for good measure. The current was slow, the sun was shining and all was right with the world. Then the float slowly sank. It had done this many times during the morning, giving a slight quiver before very slowly disappearing completely, producing the normal dace or roach for the net. This time, however, the resulting strike was met with a stubborn thump and an increase of speed the like of which I had never felt before. My clutch was spinning so fast that I actually hurt my finger when I tried to slow the spool down. If this was a dace then it was the grandfather of them all, I remember thinking to myself.

The fish shot off down the margins under an old half-sunken boat, and after about twenty yards it slowed and stopped. I could feel that there was movement on the end of the line, but no matter how hard I pulled I made no headway. We continued our sensitive chess game for over an hour, when out of the blue it gave a huge surge, resulting in a heavy breathing and very frustrated individual staring at yet another length of line flapping about in the breeze.

So far I had not actually set out to catch one of these giants, whatever they were, but the time was fast approaching as yet another encounter passed by fruitlessly.

When it became unknown adversary three, myself nil, I was again fishing for my beloved bream. I had baited up a swim at the Tags Island stretch. There are a couple of islands and I was fishing an entrance to a private area. My bait was cast right across the river and I had spodded out a considerable amount of groundbait. I had had no bites at all and was contemplating the odd forty winks when all of a sudden my dough bobbin very slowly started to move upwards. I quickly picked up the rod and struck. All hell let loose and there was an almighty crash out towards the islands and yet another whatever it was had smashed my line to bits. I can still remember thinking to myself, as I stood there shaking in the cold night air, that at least I had sort of seen this one, even though I hadn't managed to get it any nearer the net than the others.

By now I was beginning to start thinking about how on earth I could catch one of these whatever they were. So after chatting to a friend of mine who said that he had caught the occasional carp out of the Thames at Hampton Court Bridge, we duly arranged to fish this section of the river as close to the bridge as we could, baiting up for a couple of days beforehand with sweetcorn and maple peas. The night we were to fish soon arrived and we set up next to each other, with myself seated furthest away

from the bridge and Paul right next to it.

After a couple of hours and a few chub that hung themselves on our hooks, one of my rods belted off. As usual, I picked up the rod, only to find it yanked back down again as yet another whatever it was shot off under the bridge. The line could be seen rubbing on one of the bridge support columns, and as we continued a kind of pull-me-pull-you action it obviously grew weaker. Then we heard it crack. The whatever they were were beginning to laugh at my ineptitude.

There was an upside to this trip though, and that was that Paul caught a rather small member of the carp family that weighed in at all of 8lb. It was a beautiful fish, however, and I vowed then and there that I would have to catch one of my own.

I was thrashed on only one further occasion by a whatever it was before I set out to purposely catch them, and that was back downstream at the famous Kingston Bridge. I was fishing for some of the pike that inhabit this stretch at certain times of the year. This time I was using rather heavier tackle than during my other encounters, so when my alarm sounded I really bent into the fish, which I presumed to be a pike. I had captured many pike over the years, and this fight was similar to some of those that I had had before, but when the fish crashed out of the water I knew straight away, just by the sound of the splash, that this was definitely no pike. The line shot off downstream towards the bridge, and disappeared under it with me holding on and making no difference at all. I had to let it go for a good fifty to sixty yards before it slowed down and came to a halt somewhere on the other side of the bridge.

When I applied some considerable pressure I became aware that I was very, very slowly gaining line. Not much, but a small amount each time I pumped backwards. This happened four, five, maybe six times, before a thunderous thump on the end of the line, followed by an instantaneous

Hampton Court on the River Thames

ing my tackle to a heavier set, better rods, heavier line and end tackle. The whatever they were weren't going to outsmart me for much longer. Or were they?

The first major assault on these mystery fish was planned by myself and a friend, Paul Heels. We decided to use large quantities of boilies and particles to try to create a feeding area that would cover both sides of Hampton Court Bridge (some of it also ended up all over the bridge). The boilies were not a problem as at the time I was involved with quite a well-known bait firm. We decided that baiting-up would start a couple of weeks before the beginning of the season.

Firstly though, many hours were spent annoying the wife and kids in the kitchen making the bait. I bought a rather large Baby Bell washing machine with a boil setting, which helped no end in the boilie production process. Whilst making up the eighty-five million 16mm boilies, however, we destroyed a couple of boilie guns and ended up with arms much like Popeye. After many, many hours, at last the bait was finally made up. The particles were all soaked, boiled and we were ready to start our little campaign.

Every day we would go up to the bridge during the evening and empty bag after bag of the stuff over the parapet. Most of the time we would arrive at what appeared to be the rush hour, and as we lobbed handful after handful of newly made boilies off the edge of the bridge we were aware of many people watching us. Most of these commuters were more than likely thinking we had escaped from some sort of institution, as you could bet your bottom dollar they had never seen anyone behaving as we were.

Many evenings were spent watching the water near the bridge for signs of fish, but all we saw were the odd swirls from bream and chub. It is a magical place though, all lit up by the palace lights and those from the bridge itself. The whole river heaved and

release of pressure by the whatever it was, left me sitting on my backside. I was now wondering what on earth one had to do to put one of these monsters on the bank. I have since wondered whether this whatever it was may have been a catfish as I've heard that they have been caught on this stretch before.

During the following close season I started to hatch a plan to accomplish the downfall of the whatever they were. I had decided to bait up an area of the Thames with boiled baits and maple peas. This baiting was not going to be done half-heartedly; I was going to keep piling the bait into the river for three weeks before it was time to fish the prepared swim. I was also upgrad-

Andy Dixon with a perfect lineal of 12lb 10oz from the River Thames.

glistened like some huge dew-covered snake. We couldn't wait to start fishing.

One evening near the beginning of the season we went down to bait up, as we had every other night, when we noticed some anglers who couldn't wait for the beginning of the season. They were blatantly fishing in one of 'our' swims, and it was at least three days before the season started! We watched them for a while before filling in their swim with bait anyway. I must admit we did laugh for a long time after we'd thrown in about ten kilos of bait right on top of where they were fishing, as they hadn't noticed us at all. The rest of the baiting-up was uneventful, apart from us wondering if we'd maybe created a boilie bar under the surface.

It was soon time to get all the tackle ready and packed so as to be ready to go and claim our swims. Another friend came with us, but as he slept most of the session I will refrain from commenting on him, other than to say that he really enjoyed the public house, as well as the many takeaways that he devoured.

The three of us arrived at the swim and sorted out our tackle and bait for the coming of midnight. We had the normal sort of rigs – running leads, heavy line and strong hooks. Nothing new there. We did, however, use very hard pop-ups as hook baits. These were microwaved and then soaked in flavoured oil to waterproof them. They were chosen because of the many chub that inhabit the Thames. Our reckoning was that maybe they wouldn't be able to deal with these as easily as ordinary boilies. Blimey, were we wrong!

Midnight came and we cast out, expecting action from the off. Nothing happened, but we were very confident, sitting there with silly grins on our faces. As time went on, however, those grins turned into drowsy frowns until we all fell fast asleep.

Around three o'clock in the morning an alarm went off, shattering the silence with its eerie echoing scream. Paul jumped up and started to yell at the top of his voice that it was mine. I hastily looked at my alarms, then at his. I remember the look of astonishment on his face as I remarked, 'It's not mine stupid, it's yours!'

Paul grabbed his rod and it bent into a satisfying curve. The other rods were quickly wound in as we were all fishing in quite a small area, and he continued to play his unseen adversary. The fight didn't last too long as Paul certainly had the fish beaten on the size and weight ratio. Nonetheless, a fish lay in the landing net, and as it weighed in at 11lb 8oz it was nearly the same as his personal best river carp of 12lb. I still hadn't caught one. Would I ever?

We recast our baits into their former positions and sat back and chatted about what had happened, particularly the fact that Paul hadn't realized it was his rod. We had a lot of short sharp tugs on our lines during the next few hours, no doubt due to some of the chub we had worried about beforehand. Then, just as suddenly as before, it was my turn to jump up and grab some action.

I found myself attached to a fish with considerable attitude which powered off under the bridge and swirled about thirty yards further downstream. The fish, still unseen, thumped around on the end of a very long line, trying to shake the hook free, and then I gained some line. It felt very similar to the time I hooked a small rowing boat and managed to turn it round by a determined constant pressure, causing much concern to the poor bloke rowing the small craft.

I gathered in more and more line until the whatever it was was under the bridge again. Then it somehow managed to magically morph itself into one of those famous Thames shopping trolleys, a submarine, the River Thames monster, or something like that, and all went solid. I tried the usual tactic of slackening off and waiting to see if anything moved around, but nothing did, so unfortunately I had to pull for a break.

Back went the baits into the black inky depths of the Thames. More chub bleeps and tugs continued for an hour or so until, suddenly, off went the same alarm as before. This time I decided on a whack and hold tactic. This worked much better and a small common carp of about 6lb 8oz was soon staring rather bemusedly up at me from the landing net. Not long after my first river carp capture Paul was in again, and a slightly spawn-scarred mirror of 15lb-odd was joyously met by a very pleased and by now rather giggly threesome. The action continued in the same way for the next few hours, with me taking another two commons of 8lb and 7lb and a mirror of 13lb. We finished the session with huge grins on our faces, huge bags under our eyes and huge appetites for more river carp fishing.

As we had done so well on the first session of our campaign we were soon back at the bridge again; alas, this time the swim we wanted was taken. Not to be deterred, however, we decided to fish the other side – the same side of the river though. We must have looked very odd, sitting there with rods aimed at the palace like small anti-aircraft emplacements, but we didn't care one jot. We knew we were going to hammer them again and we sat whispering and chuckling to each other about how we would empty the river in the coming sessions. Chub after chub followed and our enthusiasm, although not completely cremated, was beginning to wane. I did catch a beautiful 8lb fully scaled mirror later that night, which I must say made up for being pestered by the chub somewhat, but they were becoming a problem and the hammering we expected to give the carp never materialized.

The next night we were back again in the same swim, and after a while Paul decided that he needed to go over to the local petrol station for a burger or two. I was left to sit alone and watch my bobbins and the slowly seething river. He had not been gone more than a couple of minutes when my alarm went off. I jumped up and hit into yet another chub. I played it for a little while and pulled it into the landing net. A chap and his son who were float fishing a little way up the bank came over to see the fish. I was showing it to them and watching their looks of astonishment at the size of it when out of the blue my other alarm yelled at me.

This time my strike was met by something bigger. As I had learnt before, these river carp had tails somewhat larger than their stillwater cousins, and they also knew how to use them to good effect. This one was no exception and it powered all over the river in front of me until it too eventually ended up in my net. The look on the faces of the father and son was something to behold. They had thought the chub was enormous, but now that they were staring at a 13lb linear their faces nearly fell off.

Not long afterwards Paul returned, and as I was by now all set up again, sitting quietly on my bedchair, he enquired as to whether anything had happened while he was away. I replied that I had a fish in the sack. His first reaction was that I had golden thingamabobs between my legs, but as soon as he saw the fish he just had a look of amazement on his face. I must admit it was a beautiful looking fish, and the pleasure that it brought to four people that evening made it a very special capture indeed. I think two more carp anglers were born that day, as the father and son partnership had mentioned that they would be giving river carping a go as soon as they possibly could.

Although none of the carp we caught would have broken any records, I think what made those nights so memorable for me was that to catch a fully scaled mirror, and then the next night to catch a linear too, was more than I could have hoped for from any lake, let alone a river like the Thames.

We continued fishing the bridge swims, but it soon became quite clear we had been sussed. The only bites we had were from the smiling chub and they weren't what we were after. The monsters still eluded us!

But there were (and still are) a lot more sections of the river to try. We had heard rumours of a 30lb carp having been caught from the Tags Island area and we decided that maybe it would be a good idea to try there. A couple of trips were spent walking around, looking for likely spots, and a nice-looking swim was eventually chosen. It had a grassed area with reeds on the near bank and two islands opposite. We would be fishing in between those islands, with our baits cast as close as possible to the boats moored there.

Our first session was arranged and we duly arrived at the spot and tackled up. Stringers were attached to our lines and we cast out. This was when we met one of the boat owners. To say he was not pleased to see us would be a good candidate for understatement of the year. I had aimed carefully and lobbed out my bait; unfortunately, my 3oz lead had hit one of the boats opposite and landed just over the handrail. Unbeknown to us, the boat was made of metal and the resulting clang echoed round and round like a bonging Big Ben.

The boat's owner walked over to where my end tackle had landed and picked it up. Then he looked straight at me, took out a large pair of what looked like wire cutters, held the lot over the edge of his boat and snipped the whole of my end tackle off, dropping it into the water below. I was slightly miffed at this because now there was a baited rig lying on the bottom of the river. The disgruntled owner then disappeared

A typical Thames swim.

where they had come. I did think of asking them to take my baits out and place them for me, but decided that maybe I should keep my big mouth shut on this occasion. In addition, we found that the area was becoming too populated with other anglers, so yet another move was on the cards.

I started to search for areas on my own, driving for hours up and down the river looking for likely spots. I found some lovely places, but most were either impossible to park near or there were large signs all over the place declaring 'No Fishing'. I tried a few other places on the Thames as well, like an area in front of a Sea Scout building. This section of the river was very nice to fish; I knew that carp had been caught there (seen with my own eyes, not gossip). There were a couple of problems that I hadn't foreseen, however: the huge chub. On one particular session I was using 22mm boilies and I still managed to catch two of the little devils; astonishingly they both broke the 5lb barrier. Over the next few weeks I caught four over 5lb and lots of smaller ones.

Another area that I tried was along the Surbiton and Kingston stretch, a section with No Fishing written all along the bank. There were boats moored along the close in margin and opposite was an island. I fished there one night, tight to the close in boats. My alarm went off and I found myself attached to a nuclear submarine-type fish. It shot off along the margins, with me holding the rod upside down to keep the line as low as possible.

We continued to play tug of war with each other for over an hour, the fish sometimes taking yards and yards of line, and myself occasionally gaining it all back again. I began to get a bit light-headed, being upside down for so long. Then, as usual, the whatever it was tied my line in large reef knots around one of the mooring chains and that was the end of that.

I also tried the tidal Thames as well, but, and this is a big but, you have to be made of

again into the bowels of his boat. I retackled and cast out again, making sure I missed his boat.

We had a few more encounters with Mr Boat Owner, some of which I admit were our fault, like bombing him with leftover boilies and the like from our catapults, but mostly we left each other alone. During the first night, however, a couple of other incidents took place, one of which was having a run that resulted in a small common carp of around 5lb. Another was waking up to find the Searle brothers (the Olympic rowers) sitting out in front of us, heads bowed, resting, before bombing back up the river from stern stuff to fish along the towpath near Eelpie island. There are a lot of very large carp in the tidal, but there is also an abundance of very odd people who frequent this area. One of my friends had his very expensive rod trodden on by a drunk one night, so if you are a budding young angler then I would suggest that you don't fish these sections alone. It is awesome, however, to watch the tide come up the bank, twelve foot or more, and you often get bites just as the tide reaches its highest point. One must remember that the tide does come in though, as anglers have been known to wake in the middle of the night to find water lapping round their midriffs.

So far I haven't caught any of the monsters I had hoped for. This hasn't dampened my desire to get a whatever it was in my net, however, as the fishing on Father Thames is always different. It is not like fishing a lake. The current, shopping trolleys, unknown quantities, beautifully lit up swims, and everything else that goes into river carping just make it an irresistible hobby.

The memories that go with river carping are not to be found in stillwater fishing: the time some odd biker bloke jumped into the river from the highest part of Hampton Court Bridge; or when we pushed a ghost into the river one night only to find it was a couple of drunks playing a joke; and when Paul said he could hear rain on his umbrella, but when we looked out it was yet another drunk peeing off the bridge; many laughs and memories that wouldn't have been possible anywhere else.

As you can see from my tales of the Thames, I have no real information to give others as to how, where or when to catch those elusive whatever they are fish. I will offer these snippets however: firstly, I believe that if one searches out a likely spot or two and baits up for a short while with a serious amount of bait, carp can be caught from most stretches of the Thames. Also, don't be surprised if you get connected to what seems to be the four-fifteen to Paddington; your line will regularly sing in the wind and you will never get the fish on the bank. Those whatever they are fish are right clever beggars!

18 The River Trent

Archie Braddock

I've lived beside the River Trent all my life and have fished it regularly for over forty-five years, so it's fair to say I know a bit about it. I've seen it through all its changes and in all its moods, and at one time or another have targeted every species that swims in it.

As this is a book about river carp, I shall cover the years 1989, 1990 and 1991. Although some things have changed since then, most of what I learned at that time is still relevant today. Why 1989, 1990 and 1991? Because that is the period when I fished the river intensively for carp using particles, boilies, hair-rigs, bolt-rigs – the full monty. And why stop in 1991? Because in the winter of 1991/1992 the Government started to phase out the power stations, and the river rapidly cooled. Prior to that time I regularly fished in water temperatures of over 50° Fahrenheit after dark in mid-winter; but in February 1992 I recorded 36° for the first time in more than twenty-five years of Trent temperature checking. With winter evenings (when most of my Trent carp fishing was done) now a waste of time, I abandoned it and moved on to other species. Others didn't, and expert carp catcher Shaun Harrison, whose piece follows this, will detail life without the warm water.

In my book *Fantastic Feeder Fishing* I covered my Trent carp adventures in depth, but on rereading it I'm conscious of various things I didn't cover in detail. Some information on baits I kept to myself, as when I wrote the book I was still actively carp fishing on the Trent. And for all those who read the book, no, I never did get the thirty!

Although the majority of the Trent carp are smaller commons, up to about 16lb or so, they are in fact fully grown, which I've discovered by scale reading. However, there are a small percentage that do become very big indeed. How big? Certainly thirty-pounders, probably forties, and in my opinion a good bit more. Up to 1991 they were helped by the continuous year-round feeding provided by warm water, but I doubt if such a growth rate can ever be sustained again. Still, many of these fish will still be alive and benefiting from the much reduced competition for food brought about by heavy cormorant predation and other factors.

So, how to catch Trent carp? In my book I discussed my tactics, and stressed the fact that I believed the bigger fish to be long range travellers. That still holds, but there are areas and features that always hold carp, and which I believe are visited by the larger travellers. They may well stay with their smaller brethren for only one day, or perhaps as long as a couple of months. The most reliable of these features are bridges, particularly those that have a support located mid-river. There are many such bridges on the Trent, but I shall list only those I know personally, and which invariably hold carp: Gunthorpe Bridge, a few miles downstream of Nottingham; Holme Sluice, near the famous Holme Pierrepont rowing course; Lady Flay bridge, just downstream of the city; the well known Trent Bridge itself, right in the city. This marks the start of the one-mile length of embankment, which covers two more bridges, plus a ghost

Archie Braddock with a 24lb 10oz carp from the River Trent – his first 20lb+ carp from the Trent.

bridge towards the upstream end of the embankment, where a railway bridge was once sited. Although it has been demolished there are still two mighty column supports below the surface, a favourite haunt of carp, large pike and chub.

Incidentally, the mile-long embankment is free fishing, and you can park your car virtually behind your swim. Another mile upstream and there is the Clifton Flyover bridge. I have seen some big carp here whilst barbel fishing, including a truly enormous mirror, and that was well after the power station shut down.

Moving yet higher upstream we pass two good railway bridges with mid-river supports, before coming to Sawley Bridge, my home ground, and just a little further on the mighty M1 bridge itself. My best fish from here was a mere 18lb, but I know of many much larger, including a fish of 31lb. A quarter of a mile further upstream is the Horse Bridge, the scene of several of the lost battles described in my book, and above that my knowledge becomes a little limited. My last bridge is the road bridge at Willington in Derbyshire. Obviously there are many more; all it needs is a road atlas.

The next best holding spots, always visited by the larger travellers, are the mouths of tributary rivers, streams and canals, or backwaters of any sort. Local to me are the mouths of the Derbyshire Derwent and the Leicestershire Soar, both of which have produced thirties. Even the mouth of the Erewash stream, a comparatively insignificant waterway, always holds carp. Higher up, the Derbyshire Dove mouth is another good area. The highest upstream I have been is the Catton Park Fishery, near Airewas, Staffordshire. Here the Trent is only half its normal size, and the River Mease that enters it is virtually a brook, yet the only time I fished that confluence I could clearly see double-figure commons cruising about.

Wherever there is a weir on the navigable middle and lower Trent, there is a bypass canal to enable the boat traffic to go around it. The upstream and downstream ends of these canals are also very reliable holding areas, as are the moored boats found in such areas. In fact, anywhere on the river that boats are regularly moored for long periods are carp-attracting features, and that includes the busy entrances to marinas. Purpose-built jetties with boats constantly tied up to them, preferably several boats with seven feet or more of water below them, are places which scream carp.

Similar attractions are provided by overhanging trees; best of all is a row of trees with branches in the water and ten feet of depth below them. These areas will always hold carp. Don't ignore them even if there is only three feet of muddy-bottomed water below them; I have often seen carp lazing under branches in water barely deep enough to cover them.

Any major snag is an attraction to carp. A surface tree brought down by the floods that became embedded in mid-river on my local patch was home to carp for a good five years. I took a 29lb common from just below it, and lost two other fish that felt decidedly heavier. There are many such snags dotted along the river: odd sunken barges, dumped cars, underwater walls, ancient remains of old weirs, even signposts located way out in the river to direct boats or warn them of underwater obstructions. All of them are features, and are worthy of investigation.

Even after all these numerous features have been totalled up, we are still left with a huge volume of water, larger than any stillwater in this country, and the carp do use this water even if it's only to travel from feature to feature. In my book I have described how I tackled this open water and its travelling population, but Shaun Harrison has enlarged on this in recent years, so I'll leave that to him. Suffice it to say that the sheer volume of water is the biggest obstacle the angler faces compared to stillwaters.

There is one big advantage in a huge volume of riverwater – it moves in one direction. Yes, it flows downstream. Obvious? Of course, but when applied to baits, and more particularly modern flavours, it has real significance. Unlike stillwaters, where wind direction and the consequent undertows can come from any direction (or not at all on calm days), the river flow is constant; and along with the flow goes the leak off from your attractors. Or it should do.

Even before I started producing my own flavours, my years of feeder fishing the Trent had taught me the value of a groundbait trail of attraction, how it was necessary to have different blends of materials in the feeder to achieve different effects: maize flour, for its lightness and ability to drift on the flow for a great distance; brown crumb,

141

which didn't drift so far; white crumb, which drifted even less; and finally particles, whether they be dead maggots, casters, hemp, or any of the various seeds. The latter hardly drifted at all, and carpeted the area around the feeder and hook-bait, as they were meant to.

In recent years carp groundbait philosophy has finally started to develop past the boilie or the particle bed stage. It is now suggested that crumbed or broken boilies be introduced to allow the carp faster access to the attractors that are normally locked up in the bait. It's a sound idea, but why spend time or money on the boilie in the first place, if only to break it up? A good groundbait would do the job better anyway, and you can add whatever attractors you want to it.

More recently we have the groundbait pellet that breaks down quickly to a mulch underwater. Again, a good groundbait mix will do the job quicker and cheaper, with the much favoured crushed or ground hemp used in these pellets easily available from most tackle shops. Wet the groundbait, give a handful a good squeeze, lob it in and it will quickly break down on the bottom to make a mulch carpet. The matchmen have been doing this for years, and it's perfect for short-range fishing.

At the time of writing I am fishing the Trent for barbel, and as with the carp it is necessary to have a system that can deposit your groundbait attractor mix easily and accurately mid-river, if required, and release it on or just above the bottom. I've made up my own style of bait dropper (*see* photo) which is very easy to do.

Obtain a piece of plastic sink pipe, rod tube, or anything else suitable, up to six inches long, and tape a piece of stiff rig tube securely alongside. Leave half an inch protruding at one end – call it the top end – which in use will be pointing towards the rod. Thread a piece of strong braid through the tube, tie on a swivel or ring at the top

end and a snaplink swivel at the bottom end. A knot protector bead each side of the dropper helps to prolong the life of the braid. When in use, just tie the rig to a spod rod, clip on the required size bomb at the bottom, and cast to the spot. Let it sink, a quick false strike, then wind in for a refill. It takes about thirty seconds per drop.

For my barbel groundbait I use cooked and flavoured hemp, groats, buckwheat and other particles which are dropped, still wet, into my groundbait bucket. I then add groundbait and mix the lot until it is stiff enough to stay in the dropper when casting, but still releases easily on the false strike. The groundbait mix is heavily laced with my own potent powder flavours. On the river bed there is a rapid downstream leak off from the lighter powders, a slower and more sustained leak off from heavier powders, and a fairly close grouping of the inert particles.

It is obvious that this approach can easily be adapted to carp-style groundbaits, although I can tell you that carp often do home in on my barbel groundbait, even though I do my best to avoid them! If you are foggy on groundbaits and their composition, I cover this in detail in my booklet, *Archie Braddock's Magic Book*.

The above approach is perfect for filling your swim with feeding fish of all species, which in itself will regularly pull in passing carp. It's also useful if you position yourself above one of those bridge supports or features mentioned earlier and wait for the carp to come out of their hidey holes. Yet in my last serious carp year on the Trent I moved away from this principle, and elected to fish just hook-baits with a five- or six-bait stringer and no freebies at all. By then I was convinced that the biggest fish were permanently travelling, perhaps only two or three fish together, but these were the ones I wanted to target.

In order to do this my baits had to be the best possible, with maximum leak off and

A bait dropper.

attraction, and this led me to read everything I could find on boilie make-up and flavouring. My ultimate home-made boilie was Weetabix-shaped and porous, as described in *Fantastic Feeder Fishing,* but I didn't detail my specific flavour approach then. So here goes.

Glugging, dipping and soaking were just coming into vogue in the early 1990s, so I experimented with all the recommended liquids of that time and soon found that their underwater reactions varied greatly in tank tests. There isn't space here to detail the many months of tests and results, but a fair example is the fact that essential oils provide good taste but very little leaks off, whilst ethyl alcohol flavours dissipate totally and rapidly into the water. I also worked out that locking these flavours up within the egg skin of a boilie wasn't the best way to utilize their attraction, hence my porous boilie.

To me, what was needed was a flavour on the exterior skin of a boilie, and better still a blend of flavours, to produce that multilevel leak off that I had achieved with the groundbait. Looking back now, after several years of analysing flavours and attempting to produce better ones, I realize that I was on the right track, irrespective of the fact that my earlier concoctions were comparatively crude. I achieved my aim by blending Hutchy's Sense Appeals with various propylene glycol-based flavours, a typical example of which was Strawberry Sense Appeal. It has a sticky, oily base which can be embedded in the outside skin of a boilie. It then releases into the water slowly. Propylene glycol on the other hand is water soluble, and disperses into the water much faster. Finally, there was the normal flavour level already precooked into the boilie.

How did I embed the flavour into the outside skin? By freezing. I put fifty of my home-made baits into a small freezer bag, squirted around 5ml of my above blend on to them with a pipette, and froze them. When defrosted, I would have quite a sticky bait. After each recast the boilie would be a little cleaner due to the leak off, but without totally losing its smell. The hook-bait itself was dipped in the flavour bottle before casting to make it stand out from the attached stringer boilies. This actually worked so well I generally only needed to take a fifty bag of baits from the freezer for an evening's fishing with two rods.

And now I'll come up to date. That intensive study into flavours and additives ultimately led me to produce my own a few years later, and the mass of new information I have since gathered has confirmed many of my earlier beliefs and suspicions, particularly regarding boilies. Here is the way I see it. To work well a flavour needs to be a blend of materials, both hyperactive and not so active; boiling such a flavour will reduce the active part. Put simply, heat will alter, denature or virtually destroy such a flavour, depending on its make-up. Freezing, on the other hand, has no real effect.

It follows that applying flavour to the outside of a boilie is the best way to do it, and I believe it is. It further follows that flavours aren't really fleeced within the boilie, and I believe that is also the case. There is a great advantage in having neutral boilies – the ability to change flavours at any time, without using up the old ones first. On the other hand, if you're sold on Tutti Frutti ready-mades, just freeze a different flavour on to the outside and try it on one of your rods. Everyone I know who has done this has had more pick-ups on that rod.

To sum up: fish one rod to a downstream feature, using the heavy baiting approach to draw the fish out; fish the other rod upstream with a five-bait stringer and an outside flavoured boilie to lure the traveller. Go out and catch that first Trent forty-pounder!

For information on Archie's books or flavours: 0115 972 6886.

19 The River Trent: An Update

Shaun Harrison

As I write this in October 1998, it is over twenty years since I caught my first carp from the mighty River Trent. That was during the winter period when the river steamed due to the numerous power stations dotted along its length. It was the done thing around these parts to sit with your feet in the river during the severest of winter conditions in order to keep warm. How things change!

It is not my intention to relive the bygone years with you as I know that Archie Braddock has covered this theme superbly in the previous chapter. My brief is to cover the modern-day carp fishing situation on the Trent following the demise of the famous power stations.

And what a change we have seen. Our river has suffered one hell of a lot of bad press in recent years. The big match weights of years gone by now seem just a distant memory. Many different excuses have been put forward as to why the river no longer fishes as it once did. Personally, I feel that a combination of different factors have all linked together to give the impression that it's not as good as it was. But, believe me, the big fish angler has never had it so good!

The River Trent is a perfect venue for those anglers that have been around for several years, caught a few and fancy a change. It is difficult but not impossible. There are many more pieces of the jigsaw to put together than on any stillwater: where have the free baits ended up? Have they trundled off downriver in the current? Are they continuing to roll down the river after hitting the bottom? These are all questions that I find tax the old brain more than in stillwater situations. The simple fact that the river is constantly moving adds a whole new dimension to the job of catching a carp.

During the 1998 close season I teamed up with successful Trent angler Nick Martin for a summer campaign on the river. It had been quite some time since I had devoted any serious attention to the river during the long, warm mosquito-filled days of the summer. Because of the constant boat traffic and the ever-present match-pegged stretches, for me the Trent has been mostly a winter venue. I continued to fish after the death of the power stations but things became so predictable that I lost interest. Nowadays I find it very difficult to sit it out when you know you are unlikely to catch. I am not as stubborn as I used to be when I used to sit it out just for the one freak fish that would prove a sound theory wrong!

My fishing has been very different this year as Nick has a licensed boat permanently moored on the river. This may appear to be a bit of a luxury, but can be an indispensable piece of kit for the serious big river angler; mooring rights, licence and insurance costs are similar per annum to most syndicate fees. A boat that you don't have to keep launching is so useful that it now makes me wonder how I managed to catch Trent fish without one for the last twenty years.

So much of the Trent is inaccessible for the angler carrying lots of gear. The bait can weigh as much as the rest of the tackle put together. The excessively long walks often encountered on the river to reach many of

A 20lb+ carp from the River Trent.

the decent areas can put the angler off short, efficient sessions. I used to dread the walk in the hot weather. You would work up a sweat during the long hike across the many fields, arrive in your chosen pitch all hot and bothered, then spend the rest of the evening swatting the mozzies that had been attracted to you! With a boat this isn't a problem.

This year for the first time I have been spoilt. It is a simple matter to park the Land Rover, unload the gear out of the back and straight into the boat. Climb aboard, fire up the engine and Bob's your uncle! No sweat, no nothing. Distance is not a problem so long as you have the time and the fuel. And travelling to the swim by boat seems to put me in a more relaxed frame of mind, leaving my head clear for thoughts of the job in hand.

My morals must be slowly going out of the window. Not only have I lowered myself to using a boat for fish location and tackle carrying, but I have to admit to also using a fish/depth finder this year for the first time ever! Until now I had been very anti that sort of thing, but what an eye opener it has proven to be. Stretches of river that I thought I knew so well have turned out to be so different to how I had imagined. I learned more about the river in a couple of evenings motoring up and down than I could ever have learnt from the bank.

Unlike the features Archie has detailed, I much prefer the less obvious areas. This has cost me a lot of blanks over the years. But when I do find concentrations of fish, I can milk them without others knowing. I suppose it is my tendency to seek featureless areas that explains why, despite living with-

Sunset on the River Trent.

in a couple of miles of each other, Archie and myself have never bumped into each other on the river – even when fishing the same stretches at times!

As far as fish finding is concerned, I have learnt that you cannot rely on a fish finder, however. Use them to find features and depth changes where food will collect and you are halfway there. Rely on them to signal the fish and you will waste an awful lot

of time, as well as dismissing many excellent areas. It is a trap that is so easy to fall into. Nick and I have done it. A prime example of this happened earlier this summer.

We had fished a night in an area neither of us had previously fished. During the early hours of the morning I was woken for the umpteenth time by a troublesome bream. I was just unhooking it when a large fish crashed out a couple of hundred yards upriver. I wasn't entirely unhappy with the pitch I was fishing so made a mental note of the fish for a future session. The following week, in similar conditions, we scoured the area with the fish finder and didn't pick up a single fish symbol of any description – let alone a carp! We motored on upriver trying to find solitary big fish rather than the huge shoals of chub or bream. A couple of miles later and not one carp-type signal had showed up on the screen. Darkness was creeping in and I asked Nick to drop me off in the area in which I had seen the fish roll the week before. Maybe the fish just passed through this swim rather than holed up in it, but at least I had seen a good fish.

We motored back downriver with the fish finder still switched on, arrived at the area and were amazed to see not one but several large fish show up on the screen. I set up on them and caught! If we had relied on the fish finder after first scouring the river with it I would never have bothered to fish the swim.

One very interesting observation arising from the fish finder is the fact that the majority of big fish that appear on the screen are only two or three feet below the surface. It doesn't seem to matter what depth of water is beneath them, they still appear to rest up pretty close to the surface.

One startling observation arising from the use of the boat is how close to the surface a lot of the old Trent walls are. It is possible to step out of the boat a third of the way across the river without getting a bootful of water. Yet a couple of steps either side will see you bobbing around in ten feet of water. I have seen several boats hit these walls (particularly at night). It's a wonder they aren't signposted.

One of these walls has a twenty-foot drop off. It is little wonder then that the landing of hooked fish is such a rare occurrence in some areas. Having seen the walls from above I will no longer bother to cast a rig over them; they are certainly a lot more severe than I had previously thought. The area surrounding these mysterious holes is pretty shallow. We have found a few holes which are 17–20ft when the surrounding area is generally 5–9ft. All I can assume is that these are old bomb craters. They scream out to hold concentrations of fish in big floods, yet they are out in the middle of the river where you would struggle to hold a baited end tackle in place.

It is rare to find the carp anywhere near the bottom unless you have a big bed of bait down, when they can sometimes be picked up on the screen whilst feeding. The boat and motor definitely don't put the fish off. On more than one occasion whilst experimenting one of us has gone out to check a baited area for signs of fish, found a fish feeding on it and actually received a run within minutes of being back on the bank. All exciting stuff but it can be a little off-putting when you don't find fish there. But, as I said, don't rely on fish finders. They will cost you fish.

It is worth pointing out at this stage that the few really big fish that get caught on the Trent rarely turn up in a large catch. The majority of Trent fish are shoal fish. Catch one and a few more are on the cards – so long as you don't spook them. The big fish are the last remaining shoal survivors. It would appear that many of them live solitary lives. These are the ones that I like to try to track down, away from the more densely populated areas.

Nowadays I don't catch as many fish as is possible. I have caught plenty of run of the mill fish in the past and they no longer excite me the way they once did. I can now handle the long blank hours because I know that one day it will all come right and the fish that I have strived for years to catch will finally make a mistake. Big Trent carp are very few and far between. Don't let anyone tell you any different. There are hundreds of doubles to wade through in order to catch a 20lb fish, let alone a 30lb. I feel that by

Shaun Harrison with a 20lb+ common from the Trent.

avoiding the obvious areas that produce plenty of carp I am narrowing the odds.

The nuisance species on the Trent are now a massive problem. At one time large boilies or double boilies would put them off. Not any more! The nuisance species have grown large enough to manage almost any bait you care to give them. You can end up using bait so large that I am sure you actually put the carp off. It can also be a problem knowing how much bait you actually have left in your swim once the nuisance species turn up and start to feed. For this reason I tend to use the same on the hair as I do in the loose feed. In other words, I tend to use the same size and only one bait at a time rather than multiple greedy pig rigs. I would rather hook the nuisance species. It can be a pain repeatedly getting up through the night, but I find it is the only way to gauge what is actually happening down there in the murky depths of your feeding area.

One of the best ways I have found of spooking nuisance fish away from your bait is to leave a hooked fish to kick around the swim for a bit rather than wind it straight in. When the problem species are around the carp are not generally in a feeding mood so you are unlikely to have the same effect on them.

As far as bait is concerned, my preference, as in stillwater fishing, is to offer a variety of different goodies. I will generally use an initial carpet of mixed seeds, peas, beans and nut bits. Then I like to put boilies in over the top. I generally put in different-sized baits as well as different flavours in the

149

Placing bait on the Trent.

same little patch. I no longer rely on just one type of bait to encourage a possibly non-hungry fish to have a go. Years ago it was simply a case of piling in the bait and the carp would turn up, spread it around and you would intercept the fish which would consequently find the more concentrated area of feed where your hook-baits would be sat waiting. Quite simply, you couldn't put enough in!

Nowadays this approach is the kiss of death. All that seems to happen if you pile the bait in haphazardly is that you end up attracting and feeding every bream, chub and barbel shoal within a few hundred yards. Definitely not conducive to a nice relaxed evening of river carping.

Whilst on the subject of nuisance fish, a really valuable piece of kit I now carry is a small landing net to scoop them out with. At one time I would mess around at the

edge, trying to unhook them without using my big net. I would like a pound for every time I have been splattered with mud whilst trying to remove a hook. Use a small net, lift them on to the bank and the job is much quicker and simpler. Not only that but returning fish can be easier, with no clambering up and down steep banks. I find the modern nylon meshes ideal for this job as they don't soak the ghastly bream smell up in the same way as do the more traditional soft mesh nets. I actually treat the nuisance fish to the comfort of my unhooking mat. I find it a much cleaner and quicker way of dealing with them than grovelling about in the mud and grass. Not only that but they also deserve a little respect you know!

I now like to concentrate my feed into small, tight areas. This is something that most anglers find difficult to come to terms with after fishing stillwater venues. It seems

Shaun Harrison in action on the Trent.

to scare anglers, the fact that the water moves and takes your bait off with it. Watch anglers bait the river in a much wider area than they would on a stillwater. It is as though they throw a bit upstream, a bit in front, a bit downriver, and in quite a wide band of water across the river. I presume this is so they know that a little bit of free bait will at least be close to one of their hook-baits. Yet this not only attracts every living thing in the immediate area, but also tends to spread them around the swim rather than drawing them to a hook-bait.

There are many different ways to achieve tight baiting patterns. Nick uses a pipe when in the boat or when fishing the margins and simply pours his bait down it, rather like a vacuum cleaner in reverse. I favour big bait droppers that don't release the bait until they actually touch the bottom. Others use loads of stringers.

Whichever method you choose, spend some time perfecting it. Proficient baiting will result in a lot more fish being landed. Carp will muscle smaller species off of a tight bed of bait when they decide to feed. They have got no chance of pushing chub and bream off the bait if it is spread all over the place. Keep it tight!

As far as my boilies are concerned, I go to the trouble of air drying them for a couple of weeks before use. This makes them a little more difficult for the smaller species to handle as their pharyngeal teeth aren't as powerful as those of the carp.

Baiting tight in the margins is a relatively simple job. However, it is a fact that the carp spend the majority of their time out in the middle of the river, especially if you can find an underwater snag that will give them an interesting change of current flow. I prefer to use a separate rod to those that I use for actually fishing when using my bait droppers. It is a simple matter to tie fluorescent coloured pole elastic stop knots on to the line at the correct distance for accurate baiting purposes.

Since using the boat we have started to actually place markers in position for really tight baiting. These are worth a mention as they are probably a little different to the ones you will be familiar with. They are made up of lengths of conduit piping joined with the appropriate connectors. The top sections are stuffed with polystyrene packaging for maximum buoyancy. The outside of this is wrapped in reflective tape, as used in the world of spinner and sea lure making. This reflects even the smallest amount of light from the moon. The bottom section of the marker is drilled and a large split ring or cable tie is threaded through. A 2lb boat lead is then attached to the bottom with either another cable tie or a large link swivel. This is then dropped into place upstream of where you wish to bait. The beauty of this method is that if a fish goes around it whilst being played, it simply leans over until the line is released then pops back to the surface. Simple, but very effective. Just add sections until you have the right length to reach the bottom, remembering to allow a little extra for the push of the current.

I have written several articles in the past regarding Trent carping; however, many of my findings from a few years back now seem to have altered. At one time your best chance of catching a fish was between around 5pm and midnight during the summer months. Very convenient fishing indeed. This year, however, has seen those feeding spells change dramatically. The river runs much colder and clearer than it once did. This has caused an interesting balance change throughout the species present. The cooler water has also seen an increase in many of our species: perch, pike, barbel and roach are all coming on in leaps and bounds, not only in numbers but in

size. They are all species that thrive well in cold, clear water.

The clearer water has seen the tendency of most species present to resort to night feeding only. This is one of the main reasons that the match anglers are no longer bagging. It would be interesting to see the results of a night match if the participants were capable of proficient after-dark angling. The weeklies would have a very different story to tell, believe me.

It wasn't until late summer this year that I actually managed to catch a carp the right side of midnight. This created a problem as I used to fish evenings only on the river; however, in order to catch consistently, this year I have had to resort to doing full nights. As the season has worn on it has been noticed that it is the length of time it is dark that is important, rather than the actual time of day. So long as we have around three hours of darkness they seem willing to feed. By October the evening sessions are suddenly worthwhile again.

I don't use a bivvy on the river and tend not to bother with a sleeping bag when doing night sessions. Although I do try to get some sleep in as I tend to fish sessions between work, I am always having to get up to sort out all manner of things from nuisance fish to an unwanted object drifting downriver and getting stuck on the lines. I rely on quality outdoor clothing to keep warm and comfortable rather than constantly getting in and out of a cosy sleeping bag.

So far as rigs and methods are concerned, well, carp are carp; pretty simple creatures that can appear to be so infuriatingly difficult to catch at times. It would appear that they have studied the evasion of capture for years at university, when it is quite simply us that have got it wrong. Try not to get trapped into the complicated rig syndrome. Fancy rigs invariably incorporate extra fish sussing bits going into the mouth. Most also have the tendency to tangle on a more regular basis than good no-nonsense set-ups. Concentrate more on finding the areas in which carp are at their happiest feeding. Put it where they want it and you will catch on sensible set-ups. Put it where they wouldn't normally feed and with the best rig in the world you will struggle – even more so if it is tangled.

Since their release, I can honestly say that I have used nothing more than the Kevin Nash Safety Bolt Rig System as far as my bomb set-up is concerned. If running rigs are required I simply place a bead in front of the lead clip to prevent it from jamming over the swivel. Simple but very effective and tangles are now something I hardly have to concern myself about.

Hook links and hook set-ups are again pretty standard. I use the old Cortland Micron for probably 90 per cent of my bottom bait fishing. I am not a lover of the modern ultra-fine diameter braids for hook link use, although they can be used as a main line when trying to hold a lead out in a strong current. There are no ifs and buts: fine diameter hook links cut carp's mouths. Modern ones I wouldn't use in breaking strains of less than 12lb. Hooks are tied on knotless knot style – I generally put the bait on before the hook to ensure perfect hair length. The knotless knot also allows the hair to be altered quickly. A lot of hook points are turned over on the Trent when winding in, so this way a new hook can be tied on without having to discard several feet of undamaged hook link material every session. I am not tight – just permanently skint!

Lightweight ultra-sharp hooks are not the ideal choice when big river carping. There is a hell of a lot more pressure exerted on the hook whilst playing a big fish in a strong current. Fine wire hooks cut and tear. I choose patterns that are pretty thick in the wire, but pay particular attention to the fact that they are as sharp as possible. Any doubt and the hook is replaced. Don't rely on

every hook out of a new packet being spot on.

My only little secret or special addition to my rigs is the incorporation of a small sliding barrel weight above the rig. This keeps the last few feet on the river bed to stop the horrendous presentation of a tight line festooned in weed rising straight up from your main lead.

A final mention on the subject of winter fishing the Trent. The years following the shut down of the power stations saw the bumper winter catches of the past plummet to almost nothing. The fish seemed unable to come to terms with water temperatures that they had not previously been subjected to. I don't think it was a coincidence that the chub enjoyed massive growth increases at this time; there was hardly any feeding competition from anything else for a good three months. As is the case when nature is left to its own devices, something somewhere will benefit.

Each year following the shut downs saw the carp feeding in colder and colder water as they slowly acclimatized. It is my strong belief that carp in general will happily feed down to a temperature of 39° Fahrenheit. I have only ever caught a fish in temperatures less than this once. Within a short space of time the lake was frozen over for a considerable period of time.

I have been lucky enough over the years to catch several carp through holes in the ice, yet never has the water been less than 39°. Many captures are claimed at temperatures less than stated, yet most of the time either the thermometer is wrong or the temperature hasn't actually been taken from the area in which the baits are being fished. Basically, if the thermometer reads 39° or above, I fish confidently. If it gives a reading below this then I fish hoping. There will always be odd exceptions in fishing.

I think most creatures in nature have an in-built sense that warns them of extreme conditions. We probably did ourselves at one time, but along with many other aspects it has been lost over the years due to our being protected by brick walls and instant fires. The Trent fish will now feed in temperatures as low as their stillwater counterparts. This was demonstrated to me for the first time by Lee Jackson on a long drive up north from Kent during one of the big freeze-ups a couple of years back.

Well, there you have it. I have tried to keep the material as up to date as possible without going over subjects I have covered time and again elsewhere. If you get out there and catch river carp on a regular basis then most stillwaters will appear to be quite easy by comparison. Use your head and sort out where little larders of natural and drifted food will end up and you will find carp in close proximity.

20 The River Weaver

Charles Wilson

In the heart of the Cheshire countryside can be found one of the original arteries for trade in the north-west. Originally dredged for the passage of barges carrying the region's salt, the River Weaver is a slow-moving waterway of generally uniform depth and character. Unlike most of the nation's rivers there are no dramatic features save for the locks that control water levels and protect the towns, such as Northwich, that lie upon its length. The river has now all but ceased to carry bulk goods; rowing clubs that frequently train and compete along the Weaver's length emphasize the river's new role as a recreational facility.

The river has always been well known for match fishing, with regular open and club competitions held both mid-week and at weekends. At such times pleasure anglers are required to pack up, as the river has always been run by match-orientated clubs for whom the river is the number one venue. But it was largely the experiences of local match anglers which brought the potential of carp fishing on the Weaver to the fore.

In the early and mid-1980s, a handful of local carp anglers, becoming disenchanted with the secrecy of circuit-type waters in Cheshire, started to pay attention to the match reports in the local papers. Stories of double-figure carp and anglers being regularly smashed up coupled with quiet, unpressurized fishing were enough to encourage a concerted effort to unlock the river's then untapped potential.

The first anglers to venture on to the river system did so without any background information to help them. Trial and error was the main attack. One of the most obvious differences compared with fishing on the traditional carp venues was the distances that had to be walked to reach the areas most likely to hold carp in numbers. The only advantage was that it was rare to see another angler, meaning catches could be restricted to the few people who were willing to put the effort in. The main starting places were the obvious ones, such as locks, bridges and fallen trees; in short anything that broke up the uniformity of the river and provided a sanctuary for fish. In time, other areas were explored, including the long open stretches. Despite seeming barren to begin with, closer inspection often revealed some sort of feature. Even a small change in the bank such as an overhanging bramble could produce carp. Areas without features more often saw carp just passing through, although application of bait over a couple of days would provide a short-term hit before a shoal moved on once more.

Results tended to be patchy at first, but after a short period of time some outstanding hauls were made. Catches of eighteen doubles a day were recorded on some stretches. An average result tended to be between four and eight fish per evening once the fish had been located. A blank spell for a day or an evening followed by a big hit as the fish passed through a swim was a common occurrence. However, those areas such as locks that were definite holding areas consistently produced, and proved to be the beginning of the end for a small band of anglers that had previously had

Charles Wilson with an 18lb 12oz carp from the River Weaver.

fantastic exclusive fishing available for a long period of time.

Until catches started to filter out it was rare to see a strange face on the river, but with the sheer numbers of carp being caught, news was bound to escape. At first it was just friends of the pioneers who ventured on to the banks of the Weaver, but within a very short period of time the word was out and productive areas were mobbed by anglers hoping for a piece of the action. The extra pressure soon pushed fish out and into new features and lengths of the river.

This did not have much effect on the results of the regulars; they simply moved on to other productive spots already known to them, and continued to catch through detailed knowledge of the river's carp and their movements. The fresh faces that had

simply jumped on the bandwagon started to struggle slightly. Predictably, however, the same faces started to move to wherever they saw fish being caught.

A further, less welcome side effect of the influx of carp anglers on the river was a change in the attitudes of the clubs that controlled the fishing. Where the odd discreet night in the past had not really caused a problem, bailiffs were now keenly enforcing 'no night fishing' rules. The result of this extra pressure was to break up the large shoals, with fish drifting off into much smaller groups.

The headline-making hauls that had dominated in the past had come to an end. Granted there was the occasional big hit but nothing like as many as in the past. Blank sessions started to become more frequent as the fish wised up a little. Soon the numbers

Paul Davis with a 22lb 14oz common from the Weaver.

of river carpers started to dwindle.

These days the river still receives moderate carp pressure, but not to the same degree as was seen a few years ago. Any large captures tend to be kept quiet to avoid the inevitable influx of anglers that follows. There are three main stretches of river that have carp fishing pedigree, with the Northwich and Winsford areas the best known. I'll start at the top of the river and work down.

The Bottom Flash is not strictly speaking on the River Weaver, but as part of the river system with an entry point halfway up its length it justifies a mention. Approximately ninety-eight acres and full of boats it is not as daunting as it may first appear. Over half the bank space is run by a syndicate with day and night tickets available. Day tickets are mainly on offer for bream anglers with

regular 100lb bags taken. The other half of bankside space is run by a local angling club with a smaller stretch of bank taken by a caravan site. All areas produce, with multiple catches the norm.

A mainly featureless water, most fish are taken from thirty to forty yards out, and often much closer. Experience suggests fishing at range is pointless and unnecessary. Large quantities of bait are not required as the shoals that inhabit the water will generally clear out whatever bait is available before moving on. The sheer size of the shoals makes holding fish an impractical, not to say expensive task. We have found it much better to use forty to fifty baits per rod, rebaiting after every fish. This will still see the bobbins moving regularly.

Fishing mainly weekends over a three-month period, myself and fishing partner

Paul Davies accounted for over 140 doubles, with catches of up to fourteen fish a night. The average size of the carp in the Bottom Flash tends to be mid-doubles, with the vast majority commons. Action also takes place mostly during the hours of darkness. The largest authenticated fish is a 29lb 8oz mirror caught from the caravan site three years ago. The largest fish I have taken is a mirror of 25lb 14oz which was actually my second fish from the lake – very lucky! This particular fish has since been out at over 28lb.

The head of 20lb fish is fairly small as a percentage of overall stock; however, when the mid-doubles start to come through it has the potential to be an exceptional twenties water. As with the rest of the river the problem can be location. Vast numbers of fish can move large distances very quickly.

Further down the Flash can be found the start of the built-up river proper. This is the Winsford stretch, owned by a local club, Winsford DAA. It is very popular with match anglers and competition for swims can be fierce, especially at weekends. Evening sessions are the answer, when there is a drop off in numbers on the bank. The other advantage with this is that you tend to be fishing over areas baited all day by other anglers. The carp will often exploit baited swims at the onset of dusk.

At the exit point of the river from Bottom Flash is an area we have nicknamed 'The Jungle'. Situated underneath a large round-about at the bottom of Winsford it is one of the few places I have fished where a fridge freezer is one of the features. Deep margins are the main target areas to intercept fish moving from the Flash into the rest of the river. There follows a long straight section which is hardly fished for carp before you arrive at one of my favourite spots on the river.

The Pipe swim, as we nicknamed it, is one of the best hotspots on the whole of the Winsford stretch. It is not an inflow but a three-foot diameter pipe coming vertically out of the water on the far margin in two to three feet of water. There is also a slight indentation of the far margin which promotes weed growth in the summer. In the early days we would drive past on the opposite bank, where there is a road running parallel to the river. We could check no one was fishing and throw a couple of pounds of sweetcorn around the pipe and weedbeds. This resulted in accurate baiting and also left the swim to quieten down for the hour it took to get round to the other side and set up. The action we experienced was intense to say the least. On more than one occasion it was not possible to keep two rods in the water for an evening session. Overfishing has meant that the Pipe is no longer the hotspot it once was, but fish are still catchable there.

The next significant feature is a reedy but shallow bay, which does still produce but is mainly overlooked due to the next area, a hot water inflow. This is called The Steps due to the precarious nature of the access to the swim at the bottom of a steep path. Very neglected at present, it was always considered a good spot for consistent action.

There follows a long, featureless length of about three miles which encompasses the change from Winsford DAA to Northwich AA. This stretch does produce but is rarely fished due to the distances that have to be walked to reach what appear to be uniform areas. There are features to be found along the length, but with friends of mine fishing such spots it would not be fair to mention them here.

There follows probably the best-known and most popular area on the river, namely the Vale Royal Locks. This was the first widely known hotspot on the river system as a whole, with people travelling for long distances to fish for the large numbers of carp present. The locks offer a whole host of areas to target.

The river splits at this point to include the

old river, which is the original basin that was not dug out to allow the passage of boat traffic. This forms a large island called Hultzes Island which allows access to fish both the old river and the built-up stretch, including the locks themselves. The old river is much narrower and more silty than the main river and as such has a lot more to offer the carp angler. There are numerous fallen trees, overhanging bushes and reedbeds; these in turn offer a much richer feeding ground for the carp, leading to increased numbers of fish.

The only drawback with fishing the old river is that it is blocked at one end by a weir, so you are in effect fishing an enclosed stretch of backwater. With the increase in pressure the fish present have become very wary of picking up baits in certain areas. At times the whole length, approximately a mile, may hold very few fish, with the bulk having moved out into the main river. At these times the entrance can produce bonus fish, with the carp tending to hang back before moving into the old river once more. The locks themselves are also a very good area, especially in the depths of winter. Overflow of water from the river above provides good oxygenated water and prevents the locks from freezing. These swims become very popular when the rest of the lakes in the surrounding area freeze over!

Further downstream can be found the viaduct. The stretch of river between the viaduct and the blue bridge can be noted for its overhanging trees, which once marked pronounced patrol routes of carp. Due to pressure the fish have dropped further back amongst the branches and accurate casting is required to reach the marginal shelf under

Shaun McSpadden with a winter common.

159

the canopy. The blue bridge carries the A556 Chester road and provides a holding area against the supports, but there are also other benefits. In periods of heavy rain, before the river has had a chance to rise, water floods down the road into the drains on the bridge. These in turn funnel all the water into one pipe that exits into the river. Fishing into this turbulence one summer's day resulted in an eighteen-fish catch to Shaun McSpadden, a friend of mine from Davenham. This goes to show that it always pays to improvise when fishing the river; carp will usually investigate anything out of the ordinary.

There follows a long, featureless length that is extensively match fished and often features in the match columns of the angling press. This leads into the town of Northwich and again to an area that has seen a lot carp pressure. Just before the town is a boatyard mainly holding pleasure craft. As on many of our waterways, these provide a very good holding area for all species. Fishing tight up to the moored boats will always produce, as will the turning areas for the boats. Remember that anything that breaks up the monotony of the river attracts carp. Shortly after the boatyard the river splits into two for a period of about a mile, in effect forming a large island if viewed from the air. There are locks on both sides and a largish basin on one arm. This can hold vast numbers of fish at certain times, although it can also be totally barren at others. Once again, location is crucial to long-term success.

The two arms rejoin in the centre of Northwich. This has always been a popular place to fish. It hardly freezes and so can be very busy in winter, regularly producing two or three fish per day. Far margin tactics seem to work best, with the margin actually being a floating hotel of all things. The River Dane joins the Weaver further down, the Dane being a much smaller river, at best twenty yards wide. The Dane is often a different colour from the Weaver and the mixing water seems to be highly attractive to the fish. A great many captures have occurred fishing into the turbulent water where the two meet.

Past the town centre angling pressure drops to almost zero. The river splits into various smaller channels that have hardly been explored. Lack of access is the main problem, with large industrial areas such as ICI based along the banks. There are hot water outlets that have been fished in the past, and although fishing is no longer allowed in these areas, they used to produce huge numbers of fish for the privileged few. Poaching is now the only option, and there is a lot of water further downstream still untouched and with unknown potential.

Location will always remain the most crucial factor for those hoping to catch from the Weaver, or indeed any river. The fish must be found regularly. This is not as difficult as it once was, with an increase in the number of anglers making it fairly easy for a newcomer to at least arrive in roughly the right area, simply by watching where other people are catching. This will always bring short-term, if perhaps undeserved, rewards.

A far better approach for long-term success is to venture away from the crowds and walk. The best time to do this is the close season. Our original approach was simple: drop a car off at the far end of a stretch, drive another car round to a starting point and off you go. All that is needed is a pair of trainers, polarized glasses and a bottle of water. The best times for fish-spotting are early morning and late evening, as with most stillwaters, when the fish are at their most active; obvious signs are rolling, crashing, bubbling and discoloured water. We made sure that we spent at least twenty minutes in any areas that we felt should hold carp as we found that this was not always the case.

This time spent in the close season and early on in the season enabled us to concentrate on those areas we knew held resident fish. Once these residents had taken a bit of pressure they would often move out, leading us to change our approach; if the fish were going to be mobile then we were going to have to be too. This approach relies on experience of the river as it entails moving off swims to intercept the fish as they arrive in new swims. It takes a little trial and error and a lot of confidence before you realize that you are not moving off feeding fish but that the tactic can improve results drastically.

The best times on the river have always been early morning and late evening. Due to work I have found it difficult to do many morning sessions, but evenings more than compensate for this. Short four-hour sessions travelling light often produce well. Standard tactics would be one rod to the far margin and one in the edge over a scattering of bait. The middle of the river was rarely, if ever, fished, although if a better fish was spotted moving a single hook-bait would be cast towards it without hesitation.

Basic rigs and baits work well, although under pressure the carp have not wised up as much as their brethren in the surrounding lakes in the region. I find the river ideal for testing rigs and bait for elsewhere, to gain confidence in any new methods. A good starting point on the rig side would be a standard line-aligner, size six hook, and 10–12in 12lb mono hook length. This would be best off used with a running lead. I usually use 3oz pears purely to enable the rod tips to be raised to get the line out of the slight flow affording better indication. With the leads cast on the far marginal shelf the indication is usually a sharp drop back as the fish moves away from the bank. The other indication received is the rod being ripped from the rest as the fish charges off left or right along with a large bow wave. As you can imagine this leads to exciting fishing.

A wide variety of baits work well, with fruit bird foods and fishmeal baits doing

The Weaver in winter.

well in recent times. As long as it is not over-loaded with flavour any bait should work well. I have done well on salmon, monster crab and megaspice and would feel confident on any of these flavours. The best approach is twenty to thirty baits per rod and top up after each fish. If a bulk feed is to be used both hemp and sweetcorn do very well, though mainly in summer. Although pop-ups take a lot of fish I much prefer to use bottom baits; not only are they quicker to use but the hookholds tend to be better. It is advisable to start off on the basic side as a lot of people jump in with the latest wonder rig without thinking about why they are using it. At least with mono rigs tangles are very rare, so if there is a feeding fish in the area there is every chance it will pick up the hook-bait and a take will result. If there are signs that the carp are getting a little wiser, for example rod knocks, fish losses and tenuous hookholds, the rigs can always be changed.

In winter the carp become much more localized but can still be found. Standard winter tactics for stillwaters produce, such as dipped single hook-baits cast tight to features. The key is perseverance. Stick with it and search them out. River fish are invariably a much better winter proposition than their stillwater cousins.

There is a stretch on the Northwich AA card that allows night fishing. The nights can be productive, although having hardly done any myself I do not feel qualified to say just how worthwhile they can be. I never felt the necessity to night fish, preferring short evening sessions; it was much easier to stay in touch with the shoals and you are never tempted to stay in one spot and let the fish locate you.

Boat traffic can be a bit of a pain in the summer but it is not too much trouble to wind in and recast for the bigger boats. With the use of backleads the smaller craft can easily be avoided and, if anything, increase the chance of a pick up with the disturbance they cause.

The river system as a whole holds a very large stock of carp. This may not be apparent at first, with large stretches being all but empty of fish, but this is due to the nomadic nature of the fish. If the larger groups can be found the numbers present can be incredible. As far as the average size goes, this, surprisingly, can vary from stretch to stretch. There is an area around Winsford that has always produced a better stamp of fish than most other places on the river. Just recently a couple of friends of mine took mirrors of 26lb and 19lb, a 20lb-plus common and a few more upper doubles. This was only fishing three or four evening sessions per week over a two-week period. The action does not seem to be as intense as on other stretches, but with results like this it seems to be a worthwhile sacrifice.

Taking the whole of the system into account I would say the average size would be in the 10–14lb region. This certainly is the stamp of fish one can expect when targeting the larger shoals. Another interesting point is that there is a difference between the sizes of the mirrors and commons. The ratio between these two is about 60–40, with the commons in the majority. The commons tend to be the slower growers and average around 10–12lb. The mirrors are slightly bigger at 12–14lb; however, there are quite a lot of upper doubles present. Fish over 20lb are fairly rare, with the majority of those reported being only just over the mark. Ironically, it was a suggestion of a fish twice this size which brought the river to the nation's attention.

In the mid-1990s there was a report of a 40lb common along with a 38lb fish caught in a couple of short sessions by a pleasure angler. The article suggested that these were caught on caster fished in the edge, an amazing achievement. The best bit about this catch was that the angler concerned had been bunking off from work and so did not want any pictures published in case his

Shaun McSpadden with a 24lb 8oz carp from the Weaver.

boss found out. All knowledgeable carpers in the area generally treat the story as rubbish. The fish were more likely upper doubles caught by someone who had never seen a fish bigger than a roach before and guessed the weights. This story inevitably got out to the press who went for sensational reporting without doing any homework on the water first.

There are such stories about all waters, especially ones predominately frequented by match anglers. The tales of 'they were as big as pigs' or 'it must have been over 50lb' and so on are rarely true. I would love to find a 40lb common to go at but I would need concrete evidence before I would consider mounting a campaign. In the years following the claim, none has been produced.

The biggest authenticated fish to come from the river is a mirror of 28lb-plus, last caught three years ago. This has a well-documented history and has been caught on quite a few occasions at weights from 24lb 8oz to my mate Shaun, to the more recent higher weight. This fish, nicknamed 'Ken's Pet', will probably be over the 30lb mark by now. There is very little else in terms of big fish to back this fish up. The 26lb-plus fish mentioned earlier has an interesting history however, being a former stillwater fish.

Situated further up from Bottom Flash lies a lake known as Treetops. It is very well known locally, being home to an upper 30lb common, plus around thirty to forty other 20lb plus fish. This water lies alongside the old river which is very overgrown and narrow. In times of flood it occasionally spills

Charles Wilson's first 20lb+, of 25lb 14oz.

into the lake despite the club's best efforts to keep them apart. It was never known if fish were being lost until the mirror mentioned earlier was caught out of the Bottom Flash, some two miles downstream. This particular carp, nicknamed Misery, was a regular visitor to weigh slings on Treetops. Out of its normal environment it has proved to be a lot easier to catch and has surfaced at various points all down the Winsford stretch over four or five known captures.

In the horrendous weather we experienced in 1998, the river flooded once more. Unbelievably one of the first captures from Treetops when the water receded was Misery at over 27lb. I can only assume there must be some sort of scent from the lake similar to salmon returning to their rivers, as Misery had moved at least five miles!

The question has to be: what else has moved through? A 32lb mirror has not been seen from Treetops for over five years; could this also have escaped?

There are lots of other species present in the river system, in particular the silver fish which brought the river to prominence in match fishing circles. Large shoals of bream and roach continually lead to large bags in matches if they can be located. Of interest to the carp or specimen angler are tench and chub stocks, as these can be a problem when fishing boilies. Thankfully they are not as troublesome as they could be.

The potential of the river is realistically more of the same. As far as fish sizes go the weights are slowly improving year by year. The addition of carp anglers' baits has helped with this, but the gains are nothing like one could achieve in a controlled environment. The problems lie in the management of the water. It is impossible to control the stocks that reside in the river and so working out fish weights per acre, which is the main starting point to improve growth, is a very difficult task. Add to this the mainly match-orientated membership who have little interest in the sizes and strains of the carp, and it can be seen that the future holds few surprises in the way of massive weight gains.

On the plus side there will always be a slight improvement in the size of the carp. There should be an increase in the numbers of twenties but I do not feel the river will ever be a big fish water. The potential lies in the stretches further upstream and downstream. As mentioned earlier, the stretch behind Treetops where the river reverts to its original overgrown and unpressurized self is certainly worth a look, although access is a problem. Large shoals may also have been pushed further downstream into new stretches around Barnton and Acton Bridge.

I live near the river on an untapped stretch and have walked it on many occasions. Although I have not seen a lot of activity there are carp there, if not in the numbers present elsewhere on the system. I have since moved on in my carp fishing and target the bigger fish of Redesmere and further afield down south, so I have little time to pursue these unexplored and often unknown lengths. But I do have very fond memories of my time on the Weaver, and will always keep half an eye on it as long as I live in Cheshire. Anyone fancy being a pioneer ... ?

Many thanks to Colin 'The Horse' Davidson for his help in the writing of this chapter. Thanks also to Shaun 'The Sheep' McSpadden and Paul 'Pud' Davies. The beers are on me...

21 Manchester Canals
Neil Wayte

Around Manchester there is a network of canals – a relic of the industrial revolution. These motorways of the past now provide excellent fishing for the people of Manchester.

Although primarily match waters, they now hold a huge population of carp. At the present time you are unlikely to threaten the British Record, but throughout the many miles of canal you will find fish from a few ounces up to 20lb plus. There is fishing to suit every ability of carp angler. For the more experienced carp man there is the challenge of catching a twenty-pounder from what are heavily fished, albeit match-orientated waters; for the less able carper there is a chance to bend his rod on a regular basis without the expense of all the modern items of tackle that seem to be the fashion these days.

There are many miles of canal, so it is impossible to list all of the areas where carp are caught, but what follows is a general guide to where to start looking along four of the canals. Firstly, there is the Bridgewater Canal. One of the popular areas in Manchester is around the Kellogg's Factory. There is an outlet from the factory through which the water used in the cereal production process is returned to the canal. Around this outlet are numbers of carp, which I'm told like the slightly warmer water being returned to the canal along with any extra minerals contained in the recycled water.

This is not an isolated case of carp preferring the warm water being reintroduced to its original source. The beginnings of river carping can be traced back to the Electricity Cut on the River Nene, where the carp stayed in the warmer water being pumped back into the Nene from the electricity generating plant.

Also in this area is Manchester United's Old Trafford stadium which backs on to the canal. In the water right behind the stands are plenty of carp just waiting to be caught. The wides just along from the stands also hold fish and here you have the chance of a twenty. The towpath is very narrow here, however, so you have to be careful that you don't block the passage of other towpath users, and beware of the cyclists that seem to treat all lengths of the towpaths as unofficial race tracks. Most of the cyclists are civilized human beings, but there is a minority who seem to treat fishing tackle as an obstacle to be jumped over or kicked out of the way. You have been warned!

Local carp man Keith Blakey passed on a good tip for fishing the narrow towpaths and protecting your kit. Keith sets his gear up parallel to the canal, as you would if you were fishing a quivertip, and fishes above where his baits are positioned so the line is not leaving the rods at right angles, thus stopping your rod from being pulled out of the rests when you get a take.

Moving out of Manchester to an area around Dane Road near Stretford, there are some moored boats which attract carp, and baits fished to the boats will catch. The same can be said of the boats near Brooklands railway station. These stretches are regularly match fished and the match anglers' fine lines are often broken by the

Keith Blakey with a 16lb carp from the Bridgewater Canal.

carp, so it's worth spending some time watching the match reports and noting the peg numbers where the match men get broken. Return with stronger tackle and you should be able to land these carp.

The lengths mentioned above are controlled by the Northern Anglers' Association and are fishable on a day ticket – local tackle shops will provide information on how and where to get them.

The next length is Broadheath near Altrinchham, controlled by Warrington AA. Along this length are wides with overhanging trees on the far side. Carp can be caught from under these trees but you must cast your bait either under the trees or on the very edge of them. The further you walk along the canal the more chance you have of finding a shoal of carp – and peace and quiet. Most carp anglers are lazy, so areas that are far from the access points offer a better chance of finding fish. Once you find an area with carp present it pays to prebait to keep the fish in the area. On the Warrington-controlled stretches you are only allowed to use one rod in the summer and two in winter. Don't let this put you off because you can catch some good fish by stalking them with one rod and by keeping mobile.

The second canal worth mentioning is the Trent and Mersey Canal, which is controlled by Northwich AA and Warrington AA, and once again there are good numbers of carp in this canal. The first notable spot is Barton Wide, which has both trees and boats moored on the far side, and it's to these that you should fish. Barton is capable of giving you four or five fish in a one-day session, many of which will be doubles, but it has produced fish to 26lb in the past. This is a popular wide so you may find it busy. With other people fishing it there is no need to prebait because there will be bait going in all the time, but the use of a good quality boilie will give you the edge.

Also worth mentioning are the two wides at Billinge near Northwich, one of which is known locally as The Graveyard, so-named because of the barges that sank there in the past. These barges have been removed now but the depressions they left in the bottom of the canal have created troughs in which the carp lay up and feed. The Graveyard has produced fish to 22lb, so is another area where you could catch a 20lb canal carp. The second wide is known as the top wide and is quite a walk, but it's worth the effort because it holds lots of fish, many in the 7–8lb bracket, although there are also twenties present at times. Night fishing is allowed on the wides for the more adventurous amongst you.

Moving on to Middlewich, there is another wide that holds numbers of fish but is very snaggy. With the use of either weak bomb links or the excellent Korda safety clips it is possible to catch these fish safely and not worry about leaving tethered fish. With all the end tackle products on the market these days, there is no excuse for fishing with unsafe rigs, and with the price of leads at less than a pound you shouldn't worry about losing the odd one to ensure you land fish safely.

The Ashton Canal and Peak Forest Canal is run by Stockport Federation. It starts in Manchester and carp are caught in most stretches, the most popular being the jam works (Droylsden Robinson) and up to the wide at Lumb Lane. The latter holds lots of fish between 3lb and 15lb. That's not to say that bigger fish will not be present at times because canal carp, along with their running water cousins, are prodigious travellers. When the canal reaches Portland Basin at Ashton it branches off to become the Peak Forest Canal. In the basin and on most of the stretches up to Hyde, alongside the normal mirror and common carp there's a thriving population of silver-coloured ghost carp. The ghost carp range in size from 3lb to mid-doubles and are easily spotted as they swim along the canal. They mix with the commons and mirrors. Often you spot the ghosties first and then, with careful observation, you will notice the dark shapes of the others swimming below them.

Keith Blakey works alongside the canal at Dukinfield and spends his lunchtimes walking the canal, feeding and spotting the carp. With this regular baiting the fish stay in the area and Keith can almost tell which fish will be under each tree or bush. Using the knowledge gained from his lunchtime sorties Keith has caught both ghost and mirror carp on floating baits to 14lb.

TACTICS

As with all types of carp fishing, location is the key to being successful, and apart from fishing the spots mentioned above the best way to find your fish is to follow the advice of Norman Tebbit and 'get on your bike'. By riding slowly along the towpaths and keeping your eyes open you will spot the shoals of carp. The bike will also allow you to reach the more inaccessible lengths of canal. If when fishing you get the chance to talk to the young lads who ride their bikes along the canal, ask them if they have seen any carp; you will often get information as to where they have seen large numbers of fish and how big they are. Remember that

Bridgewater Canal at the back of Old Trafford. Not the prettiest carp swim, but there are lots of carp to be caught here.

their estimates of size may be wrong but the location is nearly always spot on. When the fish are in the wides they are often very active and it is possible to watch them as they move along the far margin either on the edge of the trees or in the reeds.

The very mention of the word 'boat' makes the hair stand up on the back of canal anglers' necks, but to the canal carper a moored boat is a carp-holding area. In fact,

on stretches of canal that have no over-hanging vegetation, the carp treat boats as they would trees and shelter beneath them. Anything that overhangs the canal on the far bank is worth baiting and fishing. Even if the depth of water beneath it may only be eighteen inches the chances are that carp will get under it.

Lily pads on the marginal shelf are sure to hold carp, and a fellow member of the

Keith Blakey with a 14lb 9oz mirror.

British Carp Study Group whose garden actually backs on to the Bridgewater Canal even went to the trouble of planting his own at the bottom of the garden. Coupled with a prebaiting programme, virtually every night his effort has been rewarded with multiple catches of carp including fish over 20lb. This has been achieved during short sessions in the evening after work no doubt. So used are the carp to feeding in this spot that they have scoured the bottom to such an extent that they have cleared all the silt; all around this spot the bottom is soft and silty but at this particular point the bottom is clean.

BAIT

In the summertime it's possible to catch carp on the surface using baits such as crust, dog or cat biscuits. By looking under the trees and bushes it should not take you too long to find a few fish, and by feeding carefully you will encourage them to take floaters. For bottom fishing you can use any of the baits that you would normally use, though I would steer clear of small and soft baits because of the bream and tench. Boilies are fine but Mancunian carp do love tiger nuts fished over hemp. It's a deadly combination. Heavy baiting doesn't seem to improve your chances so stick to little and often and you will not go far wrong.

Prebaiting will improve your chances and it will hold fish in the area and stop the travellers. Canal carp will move great distances so don't expect the fish to be in the same place every time. If you can bait two or three swims at a time then you can fish them in

Dawn at the Kellogg's Factory on the Bridgewater Canal.

rotation, which will give the fish a rest and not put too much pressure on them. If you fish an area too hard you will find your results may drop off after a while because the fish will move on. By having two or more swims on the go you will also have the chance of picking up the travellers as they move from one area to another.

TACKLE

Standard carp gear is all that you will need but a rod pod will help you fish swims with concrete banks. Canal carp are still naive so there is no need for complicated rigs; a standard hair rig is as advanced as you need to get. With the boat traffic on the canal you will need to use backleads to pin your lines to the bottom to avoid them being picked up by passing barges, and in the wides it is often better to use two backleads. When fishing to the far bank of the wides close to the trees and reeds you must sit next to the rods because they will dive straight into the snags if you are not on them straight away.

As I said at the beginning, you may not be fishing for records but who is to say how big the fish will be? If you need any encouragement, back in 1990 a fish of 43lb was caught from the Exeter Canal.

Index